CONTENTS

Y0-BEN-399

KENYA

Compiled by Kathy Eldon

Illustrations by David Bygott

Kenway Publications Ltd.

First published in 1987 by
Kenway Publications Limited,
P.O. Box 18800, Nairobi.
Kenya.

Revised 1989

ISBN No. 9966-848-09-6

Graphics and Phototypeset by:
Kul Graphics Ltd., Funzi Road,
P.O. Box 18095, Nairobi.

Printed by
General Printers Ltd. Homa Bay Road,
P.O. Box 18001, Nairobi.

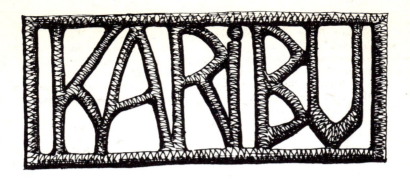

Kenya is a magical country with a history which reaches as far back as man himself. Described by palaeontologists as the "cradle of mankind", Kenya is a vital, growing nation which is home to a rich variety of peoples, and a haven for millions of the world's last wild animals.

Palm-fringed beaches line the eastern shores where the Indian Ocean marks the boundary of the nation. Snow-capped Mount Kenya soars above lush green forests and pale grasslands stretch as far as the eye can see in the west, providing sustenance for free-ranging herds of elephant, wildebeeste, zebra and other plains game.

Over forty-two different ethnic groups live together in peace, united by the common languages of Swahili and English. A friendly and confident people, Kenyans are proud of their country and pleased to share it with visitors. Thanks to an outstanding tourist infrastructure, visitors are assured a comfortable and exciting trip of a lifetime. A network of marine and wildlife parks are linked by well-maintained roads, and serviced by modern hotels and lodges where the food is good and plentiful. Experienced guides versed in wildlife, flowers and birds bring alive the country's rich heritage, offering visitors an experience unparalleled in Africa—or anywhere else!

Long before Karen Blixen wrote *Out of Africa,* East Africa was a focus of attention for explorers, missionaries and settlers, who sought to capture their impressions for posterity. Since those early days, hundreds of books have been written and now bookshops are overflowing with guidebooks, novels and stunning pictorial books, each of which seeks to portray the uniqueness of Kenya. To absorb all of them would be an impossible task. I have therefore selected some of the best known and respected specialists to write introductions to their fields. In entertaining layman terms, they bring alive the palaeontology, anthropology, wildlife, environmental concerns, arts and crafts of Kenya. A leading journalist tells the story of Kenya's long passage to "Uhuru" (independence), and other well known writers give useful tips on photography, bargaining, how to look great on safari, eating out—and how to slow down!

There is just enough information to equip you with the vision and vocabulary to ask the right questions during your stay in Kenya. Once

(v)

tantalised, you may well feel like exploring the bookshops for the indepth books and guides which have been written by the same authors.

SAFARI DIARY provides plenty of space for your own impressions and sketches. Note your views in the three-week journal, which includes maps of Nairobi and Mombasa, as well as a mileage map of popular routes through the country. There is a comprehensive information section with useful Swahili phrases and separate pages for addresses, currency transactions and purchases. Long after you have returned home, the SAFARI DIARY will remain a treasured permanent record of your trip.

I hope you will respond to this fascinating country just as Karen Blixen did when she wrote: "Here I am in Africa, where I ought to be." And don't be surprised if you're planning your next trip back, even before you've returned home. Africa has a way of being habit forming.

Welcome, and Karibuni.

Kathy Eldon,
Editor, Safari Diary

THE MAKING OF MANKIND

Richard Leakey

Director of the National Museums of Kenya and author of many books on paleontology including The Making of Mankind, *(the basis for the BBC television series),* The People of the Lake *and* Origins.

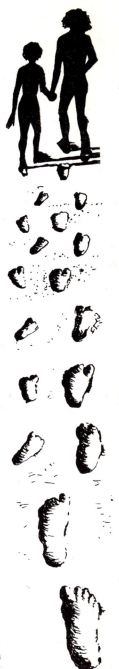

Kenya is well known in many ways, but perhaps the best known or most consistently newsworthy aspect is the country's contribution to our understanding of human origins. A tremendous amount of research has been carried out in Kenya and in the neighbouring states of Tanzania and Ethiopia over the past 50 years, and the bulk of information that now exists about our earliest ancestors has been recovered from Kenya itself. The scientific programmes have, to a large extent, been co-ordinated through the National Museums of Kenya, which has its headquarters and research facilities in the city of Nairobi. Many of the major finds can be viewed at the Nairobi Museum.

The story of human origins is long, and has its beginnings way back in time, some 18 to 20 million years ago. At that time, much of what we now know as East Africa was very different; the present highlands and great mountains were not yet developed and much of the land was low lying, covered in thick tropical forest. This environment almost certainly spread right across tropical Africa from the Atlantic coast to that of the Indian Ocean. It was an ideal habitat for primates, and the fossil record confirms this; there were many species of apes and relatively few other large mammals.

The fossil apes that have been found have been identified as possible ancestors for all the living great apes; that is the gorillas and chimps. Until 1983, it had been uncertain as to where the Asian great ape, the Orangutan, came from, but this too can now be traced to an African beginning more than 18 million years ago. These ancient apes evolved in time and it's likely that our own earliest ancestor will eventually be traced to one of these rather primitive forest dwelling creatures.

Most of the sites in Kenya that have yielded fossils are around the eastern tip of Lake Victoria; Rusinga Island, Fort Ternan, Songhor and Koru are the main localities. There are also fossil sites of this 18-million-year period along both shores of Lake Turkana, although this part of Kenya is better known for human fossils of a slightly younger age.

Some time between this early period and the present, ecological pressure and habitat changes led to the attainment of bipedalism, our unique human mode of moving about on two legs with our hands freed for other functions. We do not know when or exactly why this happened, but it was more than four million years ago. There are well preserved foot prints which dramatically show this at a site called Laetoli in Tanzania, and a variety of fossils from elsewhere, including sites in Kenya and Ethiopia, provide further proof. At present, there are very few fossil sites where one could expect to find evidence older than four million years, but several research projects are now active in the northern Rift Valley which are seeking such older remains. The most important goal in understanding and documenting human origins is to know exactly what

1

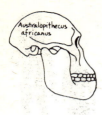

Australopithecus africanus

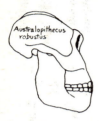

Australopithecus robustus

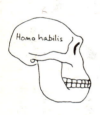

Homo habilis

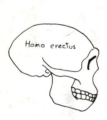

Homo erectus

Homo sapiens

it was that caused a four-legged ape to evolve into a two-legged ape. Only a careful study of fossils will answer this question.

During the past four million years, the two-legged or bipedal ape underwent further changes in response to a constantly changing environment. The great low-lying tropical forests had been replaced by bush and savanna, and many of the large mammals were becoming adapted to a more open grassland ecology. There are many sites in eastern Africa which have yielded evidence about this period, one of the most famous being Koobi Fora which lies on the eastern shore of Lake Turkana.

At Koobi Fora, there are fossil-bearing strata that effectively cover the past four million years, and tens of thousands of fossils have been collected for study at Kenya's National Museum. In this collection are remains of several distinct species of bipedal ape, or hominid, as they are generally called, and it is from these that we have learned about the final stages in human evolution. The early bipeds had small ape-like brains and have been given the scientific name *Australopithecus*. There are two principal species, one of which developed huge molar teeth that are believed to have enabled it to thrive on a coarse vegetable diet, while the second species had much smaller teeth and was presumed to have been an omnivore, eating a wide range of foods.

Around two million years ago, perhaps a little earlier, there is evidence that one of these bipedal apes began to make stone tools and so to cross an important threshold in terms of our evolution. Selection was towards increased mental aptitude, and the expansion of the brain began. Not only was the brain to increase in volume but, more importantly, its shape changed too, with certain areas of the brain being developed more than others. We can trace our 'human' traits to this event and it undoubtedly marked the beginning of what was to become much later *Homo sapiens*. The attainment of spoken language and the intellectual perception of one's own existence in time and space relate directly to the expanded brain.

The earliest form of the larger brained human ancestor has been called *Homo habilis* and well preserved fossil material exists from Koobi Fora. Early stone implements are known from Olduvai Gorge in Tanzania, from Koobi Fora and from the Omo Valley in Ethiopia, which probably can claim to have the earliest occurrence with a site dated at about 2.5 million years.

The gradual increase in brain size and the perfection of technological skills continued, and by about 1.5 million years ago, our ancestors were apparently able to manage a variety of habitats and so move farther afield. It is generally believed that by about 1.5 million years ago, humans were moving from Africa into what is now the Middle East, Europe, Asia and the Far East. Early examples of our own species, *Homo sapiens*, make their first appearance some 200,000 years ago, but it was only in the past 60,000 years that the fully modern form developed.

Kenya is fortunate to have countless sites from which this incredible story of our past can be told. Many of these are still to be studied and excavated, and the few that have been are not ideal for public viewing. There are some exceptions, however. For visitors to Kenya who are truly interested, rewarding trips can be taken to several very important site museums. Of these, the easiest to reach is Olorgesailie, which is only 60 kilometres from Nairobi along the road to Lake Magadi.

At Olorgesailie, the National Museum has provided a range of exhibits on the spectacular archaeological remains. There are thousands of stone tools lying just as they were left by our ancestors close to 500,000 years ago. A visit to this site will provide an insight into the sort of locality that archaeologists work in along Kenya's Rift Valley and is a fascinating area to anyone with even the slightest interest in geology. At Olorgesailie, a guide will conduct visitors around the excavation sites.

A similar although more dramatic (and expensive) experience is possible for anyone desiring a 550-kilometre trip north to Koobi Fora. At this site, it's possible to view fossil remains lying undisturbed and learn about the area from a trained guide. A giant fossil tortoise has been excavated (but left in place for viewing, as has an almost complete elephant skeleton, dating to about 2 million years. A museum exhibit illustrates all of the major finds of human ancestors from this region, and details the scientific disciplines that have been brought together to document our origins.

Although archaeology and prehistory may not be as visually exciting as Kenya's many other tourist attractions, anyone coming to Kenya should be aware of the fact that they are going back to their ancestral home. There is little doubt that all of mankind can trace its origins to Africa, probably to eastern Africa. Regardless of the apparent but superficial differences between the people of our planet we all share a common ancestry. It is useful to reflect upon this and to recognise that the continent of Africa was the crucible in which our species developed. The intelligent, self-aware, spiritual and technological bipedal ape emerged first in Africa, and from there spread out across the globe.

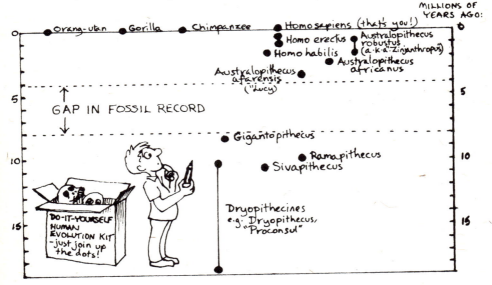

KENYA

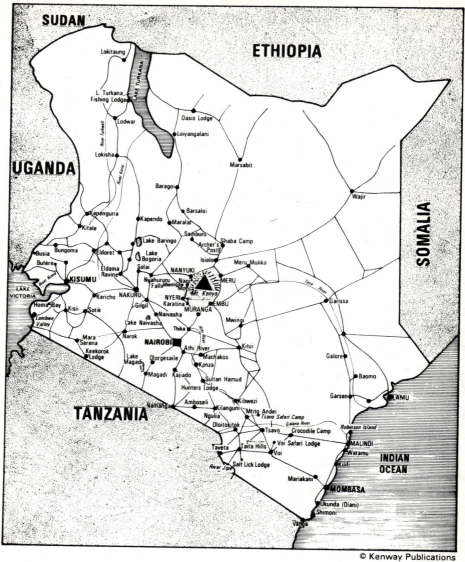

© Kenway Publications

4

THE MAKING OF KENYA

Chege Mbitiru
Managing Editor, **Africa Now**

Modern Kenya, it has been said, was created by the Uganda Railway. And yet, the land was always there—mangrove swamps, deserts, scrublands, dark forests and undulating hills, streams of sparkling cold water and the feature that was to give the country its name: the twin-peaked snow covered Mt. Kenya.

The people were there too: the Swahili at the coast, the Giriama and Taita, the Kamba, the Kikuyu, the Embu, the Meru, the Somalis, the Rendille and the Samburu. There were the Maasai, the Nandi, Kipsigis, Tugen, the Luhya and the Luo.

And there were the animals, then in millions: elephants, leopards, rhinos, hippos, wildebeest, giraffe and zebra.

However, while details of the land's interior were scanty, the outside world had a general view of what the country was like because by the time the railways was conceived, the coast had been visited by foreigners for more than 3,000 years. The Egyptians had been there and possibly the Phoenecians. The Arabs had settled along the coast from the sixth century A.D. and people from the Indian sub continent had also made their mark.

The Portuguese had been and gone, expelled by the Arabs, but not before they had built Fort Jesus in Mombasa and erected a monument in Malindi to one of their great explorers, Vasco da Gama. The British and Germans had carved out their own spheres of influence, though aside for sporadic expeditions by missionaries, traders and explorers, few foreigners had actually ventured into the interior.

One notable exception was Johann Krapf, who travelled through Akamba territory in 1851, venturing up to Yatta, not far east of Nairobi. There he saw at a distance "two horns or pillars", one covered with snow. The Akamba told him it was "Kii Nyaa", the "mountain where ostriches are," and thus the word Kenia was coined.

To capitalise on British's sphere of influence, the British East African Company was formed, but by 1894, had failed and its responsibilities were passed on to the British government. In 1896, the area between Buganda and the coast was named the East African Protectorate and thousands of Indian workers were imported employed to build the Uganda Railway, starting in Mombasa.

None of the arguments advanced in favour of the railway had anything to do with Kenya—the territory it was to pass through would change forever. The railway was needed to fight the slave trade and to give the British control over the head waters of the Nile. It took five years to complete and during that time, the British, using Sudanese troops, engaged in "wars of pacification" against the local people. Even before the railway reached the shores of Lake Victoria. white settlement in Kenya became the Kenya became the official policy.

The new settlers flocked in from Britain, South Africa, Australia and Canada. Among the earliest arrivals was Lord Delamere, who came in 1903 and for more than 30 years remained the undisputed leader of the

white settlers in East Africa. Two years after his arrival, responsibility for the Protectorate passed from the Foreign office to the Colonial Office and two years later Sir Winston Churchill, then British Under-Secretary of State for the Colonies, paid a visit.

"One would scarcely believe," he wrote in his account of the visit, "My African Journey", "that a centre so new should be able to develop so many divergent and conflicting interests, or that a community so small should be able to give each other such vigorous and vehement expression. There is already in miniature all the elements of keen social and political discord."

As he wrote those words, a young African orphan was herding his uncle's goats in Kikuyuland, not far from Nairobi. His name was Jonstone Kamau, later to be changed to Jomo Kenyatta, and he was the child destined to become the first President of the Republic of Kenya.

By the beginning of the First World War, the European community in Kenya stood at 3,000. By 1922, it had risen to 10,000 and by then, the White Highlands covered the best 17,000 of the colony's 225,000 square miles. The land was rich and had no dormant season. Labour was cheap, as the settlers persuaded the Colonial Administration to pass tax laws which eventually forced the Africans to work on their farms. Despite the wealth of the land, the settlers and Colonial Administration were by no means creating a Shangri-la.

The European presence created acute social and economic grievances which led Africans, as early as the 1920's, to demand a share of political power as the only sure method of removing the objections. In 1921 the Kikuyu Association was formed and the year after, Harry Thuku took over the leadership of the new Young Kikuyu Association.

These organisations agitated for political, economic and social rights for the Africans. In March, 1922, Thuku was jailed at the Central Police Station, where the main campus building of the University of Nairobi now stands. Africans demonstrated outside, shots were fired from the station and according to some reports, from settlers lounging on the verandah of the Norfolk Hotel nearby, at least 22 people died. The struggle for independence had begun in earnest.

From then until the beginning of the Second World War, the settlers increased their political and economic power, while the Africans struggled to develop the institutions they needed to counter that power. However, on the sidelines were the Asians: Indians, Arabs, Pakistanis and Goans. Though prosperous as artisans, shopkeepers and real estate dealers, and more numerous than the Europeans, they had been denied the political and social rights they, too, felt they deserved.

The war years saw Africans fighting in Ethiopia, North Africa, the Middle East, Malaya and Burma, after which many went back to the reserves, while their European counterparts obtained options to settle in the White Highlands.

After the war there was a resurgence of political activity. Jomo Kenyatta, after fifteen years out of the country, most of them spent agitating in London, reappeared and soon took control of the most active African political organisation, the Kikuyu Central Association.

On the 20th October, 1952, the newly arrived Governor, Sir Evelyn Baring, declared a State of Emergency. Kenyatta and nearly 200 other leaders were arrested. Early the next year, Kenyatta was convicted of being the leader of an unlawful organisation, the Mau Mau, and was sentenced to seven years in jail.

There was widespread deportation of Kikuyus from the White Highlands and urban areas to Central Province, which was largely a Kikuyu reserve. Most of these people had taken the Mau Mau oath and they retreated into the forest to fight for their land. Others were arrested and taken to detention camps. Between 1953 and 1954 there were pitched battles between Mau Mau fighters and government troops. By the end of 1955, the fighting became less strenuous and in 1960 the State of Emergency was lifted.

The Mau Mau war has been described as an insurrection, an uprising, a revolt and even as a civil war. Whatever the label, the root cause was the Africans' discontent with colonial rule. It was clear that the settler dominated government could not maintain law and order. Besides, Harold Macmillan's "winds of change" were sweeping through the colonies. The question for the British was not whether to leave, but when and how.

They tried their best to extricate themselves with dignity, but their efforts were complicated by settlers' intransigence and squabbling among the Africans. When the British finally granted Kenya Independence on 12th December, 1963, it was to two contending political parties, the Kenya African National Union (KANU) and the Kenya African Democratic Union (KADU). Kenyatta, the leader of the dominant KANU, became the country's first Prime Minister. The years since Independence have altered Kenya's two-party status, and now the country is a de juve one-party state try is a de juve one-party state with KANU dominant.

On the night of 21st August, 1978, President Jomo Kenyatta died in his sleep at State House, Mombasa, and was succeeded by his Vice President of eleven years, Daniel Arap Moi. Contrary to expectations, both locally and in many parts of the world, the transition went very smoothly. Kenyans mourned their dead President for ten days, then buried him with dignity and continued living.

Historically, colonialism in Kenya lasted for a fairly short time. In his lifetime, Kenyatta literally saw the arrival and the departure of the British. Undoubtedly though, colonialism thrust Kenya full blast into the twentieth century. Nairobi, where zebras had grazed when Thomson camped at Ngong, is today a thriving metropolis. It boasts a community of varied nationalities and races, and serves as regional headquarters for many international organisations and businesses.

The Africans, described as "treacherous, lazy and thievish" savages in the colonial days, are today in positions of authority and responsibility. Like the settlers, the Africans have not managed to create a Shangri-la, but unlike the settlers, they never said they would. They wanted a more equitable society than the settlers had established, and in this they have gone a long way.

NAIROBI
CITY CENTRE

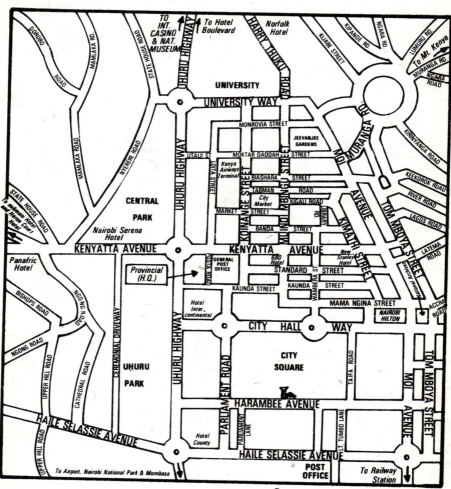

Reproduced from A - Z Guide of Nairobi
© Kenway Publications

8

A DAY IN THE LIFE OF NAIROBI

Kate Macintyre
Author of Macmillan's Nairobi: A Guide

Scatter your thoughts across this city of sunshine, colour and noise. Early in the morning, climb up to a high vantage point, to the twenty-seventh floor of the Kenyatta Conference Centre, perhaps, and witness Africa at large. To the north on a clear day, you can see Mt Kenya: serene, definitive, surreal. To the north-east lies Ol Donyo Sabuk, no longer smouldering, above the Embakasi Plains. To the south, Mt Kilimanjaro displays its ex-volcanic silhouette. Finally, to the south-west, the fist of the Ngong Hills provides the last green break before the Rift Valley. You may only guess at the shimmering heat and dust devils of the Rift, for below you spreads a city preparing for the realities of banking, spending, creating, destroying or merely existing.

Back once more on firm tarmac and you find yourself on Harambee Avenue ("Harambee" is Kenya's national slogan meaning 'let's pull together'), this street seems to pull together some of the more official elements of Nairobi. To the left, officialdom lies unmistakably in the form of the Treasury. Behind and dwarfed by the Kenyatta Conference Centre, are the neo-classical Law Courts, and a short walk to your right brings you to Parliament Buildings. Walk past the fine statue of the late President Mzee Jomo Kenyatta and in through the carved doors. Since there is nothing quite like a touch of hard sight-seeing first thing in the morning, observe the gracious Italian marble floor which leads to a mural of shields, one from each of Kenya's top ten ethnic groups. There are also some tapestries that tell the tale of colonial Kenya—'They Made it their Home'—and the seal of Independence which ends that story and begins another.

But what's the hurry? "When in Nairobi...." Walk into the centre of its square mile and have a cup of coffee or tea in one of the many cafes on Standard, Mama Ngina or Kaunda Streets. The coffee is excellent and even better when accompanied by a samosa or *mandazi* (African doughnut). But of course the value of the cafe rest is more than the mere starch or caffeine content. Quietly observe, or chat to others who may be watching their coffee or you. A deep fund of good humour is never far below the surface—which is a good thing given the interior decor of some of these cafes.

Refreshed and entertained, how about some concentrated window shopping! Cross Kenyatta Avenue, the city's pulsating artery, and move down Wabera Street to observe the Macmillan Library, with its 1931 facade of stone lions and steps, and its students (reluctant or relaxed) propping up the fine columns. Behind the Library, far more elaborate and elegant, lies the Sunni sect's Jamia Mosque, a beautiful Arabian building sporting spirelets, minarets, cupolas, inscriptions and arches, but in no way warning the unsuspecting traveller of what is in store next. The City Market rises on your left, looking for all the world like another temple. But this is an alternative temple inspiring the worship of Nairobi housewives with its fruit, vegetables, meat, fish, baskets and curios piled precariously high. Two roads away from the City Market lies one of the

9

most popular and exciting streets in Nairobi—Biashara Street, a feast of colourful cloth, originally named Bazaar Street. An overwhelming number of clothiers, haberdashers, tailors and seamstresses display their materials along both sides of the road. The choice is dazzling; the bargains tempting.

Having run the gauntlet of Biashara Street, you reach a roundabout where Nairobi's many cultural styles converge. To one side is Jeevanjee Gardens, named after one of the most famous of the early Asian settlers. The gardens are well worth a wander through for their human observation value and a raised eyebrow at the statue of Queen Victoria. Opposite the garden is Nairobi's Ismailia Mosque, whose grey massive exterior belies a calm, friendly and interesting interior.

On the far side of the roundabout, Tom Mboya Street glides away, initially to pass by Nation House and the fire station, and then by larger, more recent buildings with their anonymous glass fronts and many storeys. Stand for a moment at this roundabout and raise your eyes above street level. You will notice that above the classically-styled pavilion shopping arcades there are many pretty examples of colonial architecture: gabled or round windows, neat facades following arabesque roofs. Many of these houses have dates and many of the dates may surprise you. Visual schizophrenia could be a result of looking too closely at Nairobi's architecture, but accept and revel in its contrasts. On the eastern tangent to this roundabout, moving down towards and beyond the river, begins the seamier side of Nairobi. Behind you lies the city of office-blocks and high-rise buildings, with banks supporting resident beggars outside them. While in front of you are *dukas* (shops) packed with people sipping sodas or buying a cigarette or two. Here, the pace of life changes and the smell of spices mixes with that of forgotten refuse and neglected drains.

A curry lunch, whether vegetarian or carnivorous, is recommended at this point. Nairobi bursts at the seams with good Indian restaurants, and indeed at this meeting point of Tom Mboya Street and River Road there are a couple of superb eating places for those with empty stomachs and weary feet. Shopping is known to annihilate the soul but a curry will restore it and prepare it for an afternoon of interest.

An afternoon of "culture" lies before you whether the choice is formal (museums) or informal (the markets). The vultures of culture must not hold back. Moving from the southern end of River Road and deep into the active heart of African Nairobi, an unforgettable experience awaits you. The markets of Gikomba, Pumwani and Kariokor are for the valiant and the hardy as well as the fit. But this walk is well worth it; the venture is a highly sensual one: noise, colour and smell assault one from all angles. Gikomba market combines activity and lethargy—the twin characteristics of Nairobi. Then beyond Gikomba lies Pumwani, a world of untold tales and action. The ringing of iron on steel greets your ears as scraps of metal are hammered into pots and pans of every shape and size. Bedsteads, bracelets and buckles are a few of the items produced to the sound of this symphony. As if music were not enough, stretching away lies Pumwani proper and a wonderful display of colour. Endless rows of *kikoi* cloth hang on tangled frames as far as the eye can see. This is no washer-woman's paradise, this is one of the most striking sights Nairobi offers. Wander through the ocean of colour and you will also pass the suppliers of many of the leather and wood stalls in the centre of town. These craftsmen are worth more than a casual glance if you have the time. Maybe a stop for a 'chat and a chai' (tea) and then head for Kariokor market, half a mile farther on. This walled and eccentric area is special not merely for the smell of cooking food but also for its architectural detail. Notice the gates, the stalls and benches in the eating shelters, and take in the wonderful stone drainage system. Kariokor, named after the "Carrier Corps" assembled during the First World War, specialises in nothing more spectacular than baskets and sandals made from car tyre inner-tubing (built to last-interminably), but the drift of smoke, the bubble of laughter and the endless *chai* stalls dismiss the notion that this is any ordinary market.

Playing with extremes, return to the City Centre and, as the day draws to an end, rest your limbs and mind over a lager in the Delamere Bar at the Norfolk or the Thorn Tree at the New Stanley. Worlds apart from market scenes, here too is an opportunity to "world watch", but what a different world! Nairobi is a city of contrasts—what more can one expect from a city founded to serve the high technology of a railway in a wilderness! Nairobi thrives on contrasts; its vitality comes from a balancing act between the meditating, calm gaze of a Somali shop-keeper and the frantic suicidal tendencies of a hand-cart puller.

So, one last effort before night falls, take a friend and walk into Uhuru Park, climb the spacious terraces and look back over the city as the sun, for which it is so justly famous, sets behind you. Gradually, the glass of the high-rise is lit up and you fancy the city is on fire as the ultra-clear light plays its tricks. Nairobi is a city of soaring sky-scrapers embedded in the black-soil as firmly as the palm trees along its Uhuru Highway.

THE RAILWAY MUSEUM

Kate Macintyre

Author of Macmillan's Nairobi: A Guide

Nairobi's origins are nothing if not simple: today's modern metropolis began as a railhead set on a plain approximately half-way between Mombasa and Kampala. Swampy, disease-ridden and exposed, Nairobi nevertheless grew rapidly. In May 1899, the rail tracks reached the settlement, but within the short space of eight years Nairobi had overtaken Mombasa in importance, ousting it as the capital of East Africa. The story of the railway and the city it inspired are therefore intimately linked and the tale is an exciting one. The Railway Museum reflects the humour and determination of the men who created Nairobi, thereby transforming East Africa.

The building of the railway, "the Lunatic Line" as it was appropriately nick-named, was a heroic undertaking; and heroically stupid according to some. Those involved tackled the challenges provided by the black-maned man-eating lion, rhino and elephant, disease, hostile tribes and serious labour shortages and accomplished feats of acrobatic engineering. As one employee of the company put it: "It is good to work for the railway, not only does it help you to get rich quickly, but it also helps you to get older more quickly."

Before heading to the museum, study the railway station, itself a fascinating architectural study. Drop in to the restaurant for an astonishing trip into the past. It is difficult to decide in this "time warp" as to what is the more impressive—the starch-coated, tight-buttoned and yet cheerful waiters, or the copiously engraved, heavy silver-plated dining utensils. Absorb the atmosphere and the food. After a filling meal, the walk to the museum will do you good. Notice at one point the bizarre view to your right, that of the sky-scraping Kenyatta Conference Centre rising over a crop of maize, a poignant summing up of Nairobi if ever there was one. The museum's cool and calm atmosphere is in lovely contrast to the hectic bustle by the tea kiosks outside it. Inside, you will gaze in amazement at the variety of memorabilia, from the brass pedestal oil lamps to the fine dining table and sideboard that were rescued from the Captain's cabin of the wrecked "Koenigsburg", sunk off the coast of Tanzania during the First World War. What could be more reminiscent of the pace of life than the superbly preserved wooden bench which used to be attached to the very front of the locomotive for visiting dignitaries. Alas, the practice had to be abandoned, so the immediacy of this form of travel can only be imagined.

When you finally emerge from the museum and have had your fill of the polished old locomotives outside, don't go home yet. Walk across Uhuru Highway and explore the overgrown, deteriorating cemetery on the far side. Its headstones provide an eloquent indication of the untimely demise of some of Kenya's pioneers. "Died of lion wounds", says one, "Died while sleeping by a man-eating lion", or "John Cameron Scott, came to Africa to found the African Inland Mission in 1897, died 1898, called to higher things". Slowly rotting wooden crosses, many lying on their sides, are a poignant testimony to those who put their all into the founding of Nairobi.

THE NATIONAL MUSEUM — A LIVING SHOWCASE

Kate Macintyre
Author of Macmillan's Guide to Nairobi:

Kenya is infinitely rich in cultural matters, be they historical or pre-historical, relating to natural or man-made history. Nairobi's National Museum and Railway Museum provide living proof. Both are well presented and well maintained. No visit to the city is complete without time spent in each.

The first museum in Kenya was built in 1910 on a small site near the Provincial Commissioner's office by the newly founded "East African and Uganda Natural History Society". The society's collection rapidly grew too large for the space and moved to a larger building where the Serena Hotel now stands. The present building was not begun until 1929, initially as a memorial to one of the society's great benefactors, Sir Robert Coryndon. Since its opening in 1930, funds have been raised and patronage obtained from a variety of people and institutions, but undoubtedly one of the most important catalysts for development was Dr. Louis Leakey, a true pioneer in the realms of anthropology and paleontology. His son, Dr Richard Leakey, continues his work in the field and is also Chairman of the Board of the National Museums of Kenya, which is responsible for the expansion and maintenance of the museums.

The National Museum of Kenya in Nairobi is a complex of adjoining buildings housing different collections and exhibits, both living and dead. On arrival boost your adrenalin by visiting the Snake Park, directly in front of the main doors. Here you can stare at over two hundred species of live reptiles; the colours, shapes and sizes may astonish you, while their apparently sleepy natures reassure. The African Black Mamba (of which the blackest thing is its tongue), deserves all the thick glass and respect you can give it, while Kenya's Spitting Cobra and Puff Adder are disconcertingly referred to as "widespread and deadly". Deep reverence is reserved for the crocodile pit, where visitors are warned that "all those throwing litter into the pit will be asked to retrieve it". Twelve feet of crocodile sheds no tears on the other side of the fence.

Adjoining the Snake Park is the mesmerising, surreal Aquarium. Here you may stand hypnotised by the fabulous colouring of the beautiful Butterfly and Angel fishes and admire the grace of the Hawksbill turtle. To the right of the Snake Park lies a replica of a traditional Kikuyu homestead.

Once inside the main museum, walk left past the tusks of Ahmed and through the garden where a replica of Ahmed, the most famous elephant in Kenya, now stands. He and his huge tusks were accorded the personal protection of President Kenyatta who placed a 24-hour guard on him. Once inside the great animal hall you have an opportunity to study a collection of East Africa's wild animals, each stuffed to perfection. Upstairs is a reminder of a turbulent period of Kenya's history, the Independence struggle, while downstairs there is a display of Arab-inspired coastal culture in the Lamu Room.

Return to the main entrance of the museum and through the

entrance hall for a peek into the glass-fronted dioramas of Kenya's wildlife, still in excellent condition, though part of the museum's original exhibit. Upstairs there is an educational display of the rapidly disappearing material culture representing many of Kenya's different ethnic groups. The objects are displayed in order of their use, and include baskets and gourds, musical instruments, fishing nets and weapons, as well as extraordinary instruments for myth and magic, such as sandals soaked in donkey's urine, a useful aid in divining! The exhibition is rounded off by an extensive collection of Joy Adamson's portraits of the people of Kenya.

On the same floor is a rather incongruous chamber displaying aging photographs of the Apollo space shots. Beyond this lies what is reputedly the world's largest collection of African butterflies and other insects, all well-exhibited and labelled. But the highlight of this floor is the breathtaking bird gallery, a tribute to East Africa's wealth of avifauna, which exceeds 1,500 species. Some 900 of these species are represented in the Aga Khan Hall, including the humble starling—in Kenya a stunning irridescent blue bird.

Finally, downstairs is the section which attracts the largest number of visitors: the Mahatma Gandhi Hall, which contains a large selection of archaeological finds. The origins of man and the evolution of animals are tackled, with the current theories explained through fossils, dinosaur models, dioramas, and even a giant fossil elephant which has been transported intact from its final resting place. Perhaps nothing is more intriguing than the 35,000-year-old rock paintings that have been carefully reproduced by Dr. Mary Leakey from cave walls in Tanzania.

Following a visit to the museum's gift shop, with its carefully selected and reasonably priced items, the visitor will emerge both pleased and enlightened from the experience laid before him.

PEOPLES OF KENYA

Andrew Fedders

Co-author with Cynthia Salvadori of Peoples and Cultures of Kenya; Turkana: Pastoral Craftsmen; Maasai; *and* Through Open Doors: Views of Asian Cultures in Kenya.

Kenya can boast of an ethnic diversity which not many nations can equal. Certainly no other country in Africa is represented by such large numbers of all three of the linguistic families found on the continent: Bantu, Nilotic and Cushitic. Added to that are the European, Asian and Arab elements.

It has been, and remains, a country in a state of constant, vibrant flux. Originally there were only scattered groups of hunter-gatherers. Then came the Cushitic speakers from the north. They were followed in turn by Bantu and Nilotic speakers, the former from the west and south, the latter from the north and east. Groups of people arrived at irregular intervals, moved around, settled, or moved on, and to varying degrees assimilated with others. Cultures evolved and inevitably changed, contributing to the emergence of contemporary Kenyan society.

Kenya now claims over 25 million people representing roughly forty ethnic origins. By far the majority are Bantu-speakers, of whom there are three main branches: western, central and coastal. The western branch include the Luhya (hybrid people who consist of at least 15 subgroups), the Kisii, Kuria and Suba. The central branch contains the Kikuyu (with a few sub-groups), Embu, Mbere, Meru (also with several sub-groups). The coastal branch comprises the Mijikenda ("nine villages") of sub-groups such as the Giriama, Pokomo and Riverine group, the Malakote and Swahili, who according to some scholars embrace the Bajani, according to others, not. Taveta are slotted between the central and coastal branches.

In general, Bantu speakers are primarily agriculturlists, particularly the Luhya of western province, the Kisii of Nyanza, the Kikuyu, Embu and Meru of the central highlands, and the Mijikenda and Taita of coast province. Because of the nature of their habitats, the Mbere, Tharaka and Kamba accentuate the animal husbandry aspect of their mixed agricultural economies. Fishing is an important factor in the economies of the Suba on the islands near Homa Bay, the Pokomo along the Tana, the Taveta by Lake Jipe, and the Bajuni of Mamba and Swahili have long engaged in trade.

Examples of Bantu-speakers' material culture which leap most readily to the visitor's eyes are Kisii soapstone carvings and bead-encrusted stools, Kamba woodcarvings (not a traditional craft), furniture from the Bajun islands and a vast variety of baskets.

Next in numbers are the Nilotic speakers. There are three main branches: western (or river-lake) southern (or highland) and eastern (or plains). The Ino are the only representatives of the western branch. The southern branch consists of the Kalenjin groups: the Kipsigis, Nandi, Tugen, Elgeyo, Marakwet and Pokot. There are some more smaller groups clustered around Mount Elgon as well. The western branch has two divisions: Teso-Turkana of the Teso and Turkana, and Maa, which

includes the Maasai, Njemps and Samburu.

Traditionally, except for the Teso who live by the Uganda border, these have been cattle cultures, although today only the Plains Pokot, Turkana, Maasai and Samburu follow a primarily pastoral lifestyle. Most Turkana, some Pokot and a few Samburu keep camels in addition to cattle. The Kalenjin groups of the western highlands and the Luo of Nyanza have, over the course of time, become increasingly involved in cultivation.

In the past it was appropriate to describe many of the Nilotic speakers as pastoralists who practised agriculture, but today it is more fitting to describe many of them as agriculturlists who practise pastoralism. Nevertheless, the ritual as well as practical value placed on livestock remains incalculable.

Among the pastoralists, material culture is restricted to essential items: a mobile lifestyle curtails the carting around of needless encumbrances. Ornaments and ornamentation, however, are essential for them. Hence the lavish use of beads and bangles on both bodies and possessions. Objects of Nilotic-speaker beadwork are items which a visitor may well want to take home as a souvenir.

Then there are the Cushitic-speaking peoples. They have two branches: the sprawling eastern of Kenya's mostly arid regions and the minuscule southern of the lowermost Tana. Northern peoples are represented by the Shangila, Galla and other similar pastoralists.

The Galla, Boni and Dahalo have traditionally been hunter-gatherers, although only marginally so today. The El Molo, only a few hundred people, form a somewhat disparate community: they fish on Lake Turkana and keep miniature lake-weed grazing cattle on the shore. These groups are associated with Cushitic-speaking pastoralists in much the same way that the Ndorobo and Okiek are with the Maasai and Kalenjin-speakers. Like the El Molo, the Burji defy convenient categorisation: they are Marsabit's dominant merchant community and have a long tradition as weavers.

Acquiring items of their material cultures will be a bit difficult: for one thing, Cushitic-speakers are not easily accessible to the two-week safari tripper. Nevertheless, the body ornaments are very attractive and the water containers are exquisite.

Common "European" tribes are also represented in Kenya: old settlers, old Kenya-hands, eager expatriates on two-year contracts and all manner of package tourists.

Asians, particularly from the Punjab and Gujarat region of India are found in great numbers; Hindus, Muslims, Jains, Sikhs and multitudes of smaller communities. They, too, have contributed considerably to the total culture of the country.

The cultural mixture which is Kenya gives the country a sense of vitality and energy which is unique on the continent of Africa.

16

EXPLORING KENYA'S PARKS AND RESERVES

Michael Gore
Diplomat, wildlife photographer and author of On Safari in Kenya

On a quiet night, people living in the western suburbs of Nairobi can still hear the deep roar of lions as they challenge each other across the Athi Plains. The lions live in the Nairobi Game Park, a unique and wild refuge which borders the modern capital city. It is here that many visitors receive their first introduction to Kenya's spectacular wildlife.

Nairobi National Park is one of more than 30 areas which have been set aside by the Kenya government to preserve what remains of the teeming wildlife which once roamed freely across the African savanna. Other parks and reserves protect the threatened coral reefs and marine life along the Kenya coast.

Kenya can boast both the largest and the smallest national parks in Africa. Tsavo covers 20,500 square kilometres, making it larger than the state of Israel; Saiwa Swamp, half way between Kitale and Kapenguria, is just 1.9 square kilometres and was established specifically to protect the rare sitatunga, a large, handsome antelope which spends most of the time partly submerged, hidden amidst floating vegetation.

In several of the parks it is still possible to see animals in the vast numbers which astounded early explorers a century ago. Herds of several hundred elephant are not unusual at Tsavo and Amboseli—well over a million wildebeest and zebra spread over the plains as far as the eye can see at the Maasai Mara reserve during their annual migration into Kenya from the Serengeti—a million lesser flamingos feed in the shallows of Lake Nakuru—and even in Nairobi National Park there may be as many as 50,000 large ungulates (hooved animals) gathered together at the end of a particularly dry season when the waterholes on the Athi Plains have evaporated.

Kenya's parks encompass every type of habitat found in this varied and beautiful land. All of Mt Kenya above 3,355 metres, a total of 715 square kilometres, is a national park—elephant and buffalo lurk in the bamboo forest, while melanistic leopard, serval cat, antelope and little-known birds are found on the alpine moorland below the twin peaks of Batian and Nelion.

Similarly, the Aberdare National Park covers the higher slopes of the Aberdare mountain range with a narrow strip, the Salient, stretching 20 kilometres down the eastern slopes almost to Nyeri. Two unique hotels, Treetops and the Ark, overlook salt licks in the Salient. Here elephants, black rhinos, buffalo and a host of small animals can be seen at close range throughout the night as they drink and enjoy the salt lick beneath an artificial moon. Leopard are regularly seen around these hotels, as are Giant Forest Hogs, one of the mammals most recently discovered. Despite their impressive size and the fact that they are quite common in the Salient, they were not described until 1904.

No wildlife safari in Kenya is complete without a visit to Amboseli National Park. For there, with just a little luck, the visitor will see elephant, lion, cheetah and the endangered black rhinoceros all in a

17

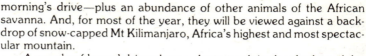

morning's drive—plus an abundance of other animals of the African savanna. And, for most of the year, they will be viewed against a backdrop of snow-capped Mt Kilimanjaro, Africa's highest and most spectacular mountain.

A couple of hours' drive along a dusty track in the shadow of the mountain takes the visitor to Tsavo National Park. Over the years, elephant and bush fires have changed Tsavo by destroying most of the trees, but the park is so vast, and particularly the western sector so beautiful, that there is always plenty to see. At Mzima Springs, resident hippos, attended by shoals of barbels, may be watched from an underwater observation chamber as they cavort on the riverbed. And no one should leave Kenya without seeing Tsavo's red elephants.

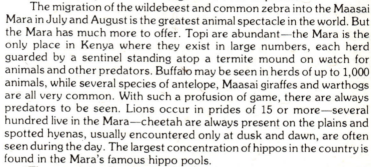

The migration of the wildebeest and common zebra into the Maasai Mara in July and August is the greatest animal spectacle in the world. But the Mara has much more to offer. Topi are abundant—the Mara is the only place in Kenya where they exist in large numbers, each herd guarded by a sentinel standing atop a termite mound on watch for animals and other predators. Buffalo may be seen in herds of up to 1,000 animals, while several species of antelope, Maasai giraffes and warthogs are all very common. With such a profusion of game, there are always predators to be seen. Lions occur in prides of 15 or more—several hundred live in the Mara—cheetah are always present on the plains and spotted hyenas, usually encountered only at dusk and dawn, are often seen during the day. The largest concentration of hippos in the country is found in the Mara's famous hippo pools.

There are a number of parks and reserves in northern Kenya, a vast area of desert and semi-desert which used to be called the Northern Frontier District. Best known and most frequently visited are the Samburu-Buffalo Springs reserves and Meru National Park. These northern parks provide a sanctuary for several animals not easily seen elsewhere in Kenya. There, reticulated giraffe replace the familiar Maasai giraffe of southern parks and the delicately marked Grevy's zebra occur rather than the common zebra. Beisa oryx and gerenuk are two animals which have adapted to living in semi-arid conditions—both are quite common. Joy Adamson rehabilitated Elsa the lioness at Meru.

Several stretches of the Kenya coast have been designated as national parks to protect the shells and corals which were being removed as souvenirs. Malindi and Watamu Marine Parks are among the finest and most easily accessible places on earth to enjoy the spendour of the teeming life of a coral reef.

Kenya's national parks and reserves are of critical importance to the survival of many specis of animals. This would be sufficient reason for ensuring that they remain inviolate. But they are also essential to the country's economy, for tourism is the largest source of foreign exchange and it is the wildlife, even more than the beautiful beaches, which attract hundreds of thousands of overseas visitors to Kenya every year.

BLACK RHINOS: AN UNCERTAIN FUTURE

Chryssee Perry Martin

Editor of the Kenya Museum Society's Journal, Kenya Past and Present, *and co-author with her husband of* Run, Rhino, Run.

Twenty years ago visitors to Kenya rarely paid much attention to black rhinos. The animals usually made a nuisance of themselves, charging unexpectedly through the bushes of parks, interrupting bird-watching or disturbing other animals at waterholes. They were regarded as rather stupid beasts, with little personality and less beauty. A friend of mine wrote a book in the 1960s for American tourists, stating: "Gawd, if you've seen one rhino, you've seen 'em all!"

Today, it's a different story. Second only to lions on the list of animals visitors most want to see are rhinos. However, between 1970 and 1984, East Africa lost 90% of its rhino population. In the 1960's there were 7,000 rhinos in Tsavo alone—Kenya now boasts less than 500 for the whole country. Many rhinos succumbed to the terrible drought of 1971, and actually starved to death. Most others fell to poisoned arrows and bullets from a range of rifles that included Kalashnikovs. Where rhinos had once lived, there now lay rotting carcasses with great, gaping holes in their foreheads where the horns had been hacked away.

Pundits claimed the poaching was due to a demand in the Far East for rhino horn as an aphrodisiac. Neither my husband, Esmond (a geographer with a penchant for studying smuggling in the Indian Ocean) nor I quite believed such a fanciful explanation. We thought it could be possible that a country with a traditional demand of some sort for rhino horn might suddenly want much more rhino horn, but we didn't have any idea why until October 1978 when I was dragging Esmond through a maze of little shops in the souk of Sana'a, North Yemen.

One of the poorest countries of the world, North Yemen had been closed to the outside world and ruled by the whims of autocratic imams until civil war broke out in 1962. Very few Yemenis had ever been outside their own country, but when that war ended some eight years later, many Yemeni men went to Saudi Arabia and other Gulf States to work on construction sites. Suddenly, the impact of the 20th century was upon them. They became part of the monied economy, and by 1978 they were able to send back home the equivalent of three million dollars a day from their migrant jobs. They were in a position to buy all the things they wanted. Among other coveted possessions were daggers with rhino horn handles—formerly the status symbol of the imams and their cronies, and very limited in number.

Poking around one of the jewellery stalls in the medieval-looking souk, Esmond and I came across a dagger with a rhino horn handle; being so excited about seeing it, we asked to be led to the dagger-making area and found innumerable stashes of relatively new rhino horn that would soon be cut and carved into handles. A large section of the souk specialized entirely in meeting the demand for daggers with rhino horn handles. Almost as fast as they were being made, the daggers were sold.

Between 1972 and 1978 North Yemen imported about 28 tonnes of rhino horn, approximately 40% of all the horn on the market. It was the

19

huge demand of the Yemenis for rhino horn that pushed up its price to $500 a kilo by 1979. It's not surprising, therefore, that elephant poachers switched to hunting rhinos as a more lucrative enterprise. Besides, it's a lot easier to kill a rhino than an elephant, and to hide a rhino horn is a cinch in comparison to an ivory tusk.

Now almost all rhino horn moving across one international boundary to another is illegal. However, customs authorities rarely confiscate shipments. Most of them wouldn't recognise a rhino horn in the first place, even though it's quite unlike any other horn, being solid and composed of hairlike particles. When artistically carved, rhino horn takes on a translucence like amber and can be truly beautiful. During the Ming Dynasty in China, exquisite trinkets carved from African rhino horn were given to the Emperors for their birthdays.

Traditionally, it is mainly the Chinese-speaking peoples who have wanted rhino horn. Today, they buy about half of all the rhino horn marketed. When the prices sky-rocketed in the 1970s, Southeast Asian economies were booming and the Chinese from Taiwan, Malaysia, Indonesia, Singapore, Hong Kong, Macao and Thailand were still able to compete for supplies, and so were the Japanese and South Koreans who also use rhino horn.

Esmond and I have spent several years studying the international trade in rhino products; we have found that the main use for rhino horn is medicinal. The Chinese (and other Asians who have come under Chinese influence in the past) believe that rhino horn is capable of curing a multitude of human ailments. In many parts of Asia, it is used as an aspirin to cure anything from simple headaches to dangerously common ailments. Rhino horn can be purchased in the form of tonics, tablets and powders.

Surprisingly to many, aside from a few Gujaratis in one part of India, none of the consumers of rhino horn consider it to be a love potion. In Esmond's and my book, *Run, Rhino, Run* (London: Chatto & Windus, 1982), we tell the story of how westerners came to believe in the myth that the Chinese use rhino horn as an aphrodisiac.)

The rhino will be threatened as long as there is a widespread demand for its horn. Frankly, it does not matter whether the demand is for dagger handles or medicine; what must be done is to counter that demand with acceptable substitutes in order to protect the remaining rhinos. This is what we are working on now. The government of Kenya is concerned about its rhino losses and wants to safeguard as many rhinos as possible from poachers. A great deal of money, manpower and equipment is being invested to this end. Isolated rhinos are being translocated into selected areas of private ranches, reserves and parks. Anti-poaching techniques are being improved, and there is a hue and cry for stricter law enforcement. The attempts at setting up breeding centres for rhinos are all being made to repopulate Kenya's parks with their offspring. Let's hope that this may become possible. It would be very sad if the only rhinos left in Kenya were those kept in enclosures behind electric fences.

CAN THE GAME CONTINUE?

Dr. David Western

Wildlife biologist, Fellow of the New York Zoological Society and author of A Wildlife Guide and a Natural History of Amboseli

Kenya's national parks and reserves attract nearly 600,000 visitors each year—most of them from overseas, nearly all drawn by the promise of unspoilt nature and countless animals. However, although Kenya's wild areas are more natural than most, even they have been strongly influenced by human activity, whether fire, livestock or hunting—and even by tourism. It is quite likely that 'East African savannas have been influenced by hunter-gatherers for more than two million years and have been extensively changed by pastoralists in the past three thousand years. Before the first national parks were established in the 1940s, it was impossible to find any region totally devoid of human activity. Ironically, then, what we see in Kenya's parks today is not entirely natural, but bears a distinctly human influence, albeit one which has not lessened the beauty of the savannas.

Hunting and gathering was man's way of life from the time our species became recognisably human more than two million years ago until around 10,000 years ago, when agriculture began.

Although those societies existed at very low population densities we know they had a profound effect on wildlife. The extinction of dozens of Eurasian and American mammals during the past 20,000 years was due largely to human hunting. Though people exterminated fewer animals in Africa, their influence was still strong, especially through the widespread use of fire, which helped create the present savannas.

Until a few thousand years ago, Kenya had less than 100,000 people. Their well-being was linked to that of wildlife and wild vegetation—they followed herds and pastures, and wherever they over-hunted or over-harvested, they were forced to move on. But in recent millenia, the adoption of cultivation and the introduction of domestic stock changed that relationship from dependency to competition. Wildlife is inimical to cultivation and was inevitably driven out wherever crops were planted. However, beyond the confines of the small-holding, farmers still hunted and had some use for wildlife. Because farmers practised shifting cultivation, wildlife continually reoccupied abandoned plots. As populations increased and switched to sedentary agriculture, wildlife became increasingly displaced and, by the turn of the century, was absent from the heavily populated regions of western Kenya. By the 1980s, Kenya's population exceeded 19 million people, most of them farmers, and there was little space left in the agricultural areas for wildlife. Not surprisingly, few of today's Kenyans have ever seen wildlife, or know much about animals.

The situation was different over most of Kenya because the land was too arid for agriculture and was occupied by pastoralists like the Maasai, Samburu, Turkana and Orma, who depended on the milk and meat of their livestock. Wildlife persisted in the pastoral areas, partly because animals were difficult for herders to eradicate and partly because during droughts prior to colonial times, game served as a meat

"GREAT-GREAT-GRANDPA WAS FOOD FOR THE LOCAL PEOPLE..."

"GREAT-GRANDPA WAS SPORT FOR THE SETTLERS..."

"GRANDPA WAS AGRICULTURAL VERMIN..."

KEEP OUT.

"PAPA WAS AN AESTHETIC RESOURCE, EARNING FOREIGN EXCHANGE..."

GNU — MARA 1975

"SO WHAT'S GNU FOR ME?"

supplement. Having to compete with wild grazing animals for pasture, having to periodically rely on them as "second" cattle and having to protect their herds from predators made the pastoralists keenly aware of wildlife and extremely knowledgeable about it.

The British colonial government changed the wildlife-people balance when it introduced new laws shortly before the turn of the century. In making wildlife into State rather than common property, government denied the people their traditional hunting rights. Although the new laws temporarily protected wildlife from overhunting (made possible by the introduction of modern firearms), they caused considerable local resentment. Of whatever practical use wildlife had been before was suddenly irrelevant and hunters who had traditionally killed animals for food were branded as poachers and criminally prosecuted. The laws were interpreted as a method of protecting wildlife for the colonists, denying indigenous people their rights to the game and protection from it. This view was fuelled further, given that the colonial settlers hunted game and greatly reduced wildlife wherever they established their own farms. Wildlife in the drier regions was fortunately spared and to protect what was now recognised as a valuable but endangered asset, national parks and reserves were established from the 1940s onwards. They now cover 7% of Kenya. Inevitably their creation meant the displacement of people, mostly pastoralists who still held land communally rather than individually. The land grab caused further resentment, for it was difficult for the herder or farmer to appreciate why land was reserved exclusively for wildlife when it was in short supply for people, and why animals should continue to wander freely. It is that antagonism towards wildlife which threatens wildlife today, even in the national parks, for few animals will survive unless the vast herds retain access to their migratory routes, which today are largely on ranches.

Fortunately, despite the strong feelings that were developed against wildlife, the situation has recently begun to look more hopeful. Kenya has become a wildlife mecca for overseas tourists as well as for the small but fast growing number of its own citizens. The parks and the revenues earned by them have helped win increasing government and private sector support for wildlife and, no doubt, will continue to do so as more Kenyans can afford the visits and begin to appreciate wildlife. But that doesn't solve the more important issue of what to do with local residents around the parks who believe they suffer unfairly at the hands of the government and outside visitors. To redress this inbalance the government recently changed wildlife laws to permit land owners to benefit from wildlife in a variety of ways—through tourist campsite and lodge revenues, through social services and through various forms of wildlife utilisation. In areas such as Amboseli and the Mara, where different incentive schemes have been established, attitudes have quickly become more favourable to wildlife and give considerable hope that, in future, animals will continue to occupy the land outside parks. Added to the commitment Kenya already has to national parks, there is reason to hope that vested self-interest among land owners will re-establish the age-old interdependency between man and beast and guarantee a safe future for Kenya's wildlife.

A BIRD'S-EYE VIEW OF KENYA

John Karmali

Fellow of the Royal Photographic Society, Chairman of the Governing Board of the National Museums of Kenya and author of Birds of Africa *and* Beautiful Birds of Kenya

Kenya is rightly proud of its great variety of wildlife, and of the relative ease with which it can be seen. Animals in their natural habitat have always provided a strong attraction for visitors, but in recent years more and more travellers have become aware of the astonishing numbers of colourful birds that are to be found in Kenya.

Of an estimated 9,000 bird species in the world, Africa south of the Sahara can boast about 1,750. The figure for East Africa (made up of Kenya, Uganda and Tanzania) is 1,293 species and Kenya alone is represented by approximately 1,045. This makes it the country with the richest avifauna on the African continent.

Any keen birdwatcher who visits Kenya has a chance to see 60% of Africa's avifauna, while anyone who can range over Uganda and Tanzania as well can make that figure 74%. Even an observer confined to a 25-mile radius of Nairobi has the chance of seeing over 50% of Kenya's birds. For an individual to count over 100 species in a day's outing is not all that difficult, if somewhat strenuous. The one-day record in Kenya is 248 species, a good indication of the visibility of bird varieties.

So what makes East Africa, and in particular Kenya, so special? From a global perspective, geographical distribution of species is determined by a variety of factors. These include the physical structure of the land-mass and its natural features; the climate and its effect on vegetation; and the presence of competitive species in areas which are otherwise easy of access and suitable. So let us look at East Africa, bearing these in mind.

The physical geography is complicated and highly diversified, extending as it does from sea level to high mountains. A typical continental shelf type of coastal plain is generally absent from the East African seaside. Farther west, immediately beyond the coastal belt, an extensive plateau rises very gradually to about 3,000 feet and covers a large part of northern Kenya, including Wajir. To the south of Mombasa, Tanga and beyond, this zone continues as a narrow belt, but expands below Morogoro to include much of south-eastern Tanzania.

The greater part of Uganda and Tanzania forms a large interior plateau varying between 2,000 and 6,000 feet. This continues in parts of Kenya northeast of Moshi through a wide fringe crossing the Athi River east of Nairobi and running northwards as a much narrower belt.

Much of central Kenya, the northern and southern highlands of Tanzania, southwestern Uganda and the Ruwenzori Mountains rise above 4,500 feet, the highest points being Mount Kenya (17,040 feet) and Mount Kilimanjaro (19,340 feet). These areas form a distinct contrast to the surrounding lower plateau. Finally, a number of lakes, small and large, alkaline and freshwater, exist along the floor of the East African Rift Valley.

East Africa's climate is equally varied, though the only aspect which

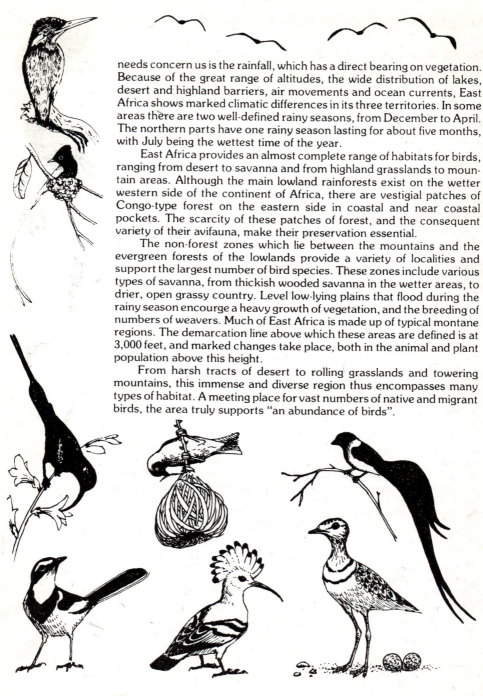

needs concern us is the rainfall, which has a direct bearing on vegetation. Because of the great range of altitudes, the wide distribution of lakes, desert and highland barriers, air movements and ocean currents, East Africa shows marked climatic differences in its three territories. In some areas there are two well-defined rainy seasons, from December to April. The northern parts have one rainy season lasting for about five months, with July being the wettest time of the year.

East Africa provides an almost complete range of habitats for birds, ranging from desert to savanna and from highland grasslands to mountain areas. Although the main lowland rainforests exist on the wetter western side of the continent of Africa, there are vestigial patches of Congo-type forest on the eastern side in coastal and near coastal pockets. The scarcity of these patches of forest, and the consequent variety of their avifauna, make their preservation essential.

The non-forest zones which lie between the mountains and the evergreen forests of the lowlands provide a variety of localities and support the largest number of bird species. These zones include various types of savanna, from thickish wooded savanna in the wetter areas, to drier, open grassy country. Level low-lying plains that flood during the rainy season encourge a heavy growth of vegetation, and the breeding of numbers of weavers. Much of East Africa is made up of typical montane regions. The demarcation line above which these areas are defined is at 3,000 feet, and marked changes take place, both in the animal and plant population above this height.

From harsh tracts of desert to rolling grasslands and towering mountains, this immense and diverse region thus encompasses many types of habitat. A meeting place for vast numbers of native and migrant birds, the area truly supports "an abundance of birds".

24

THE FLOWERS AND THE TREES

Sir Michael Blundell
Author of The Wild Flowers of Kenya

Sixty years ago, as a very young man, my daily task·was to ride on horseback over more than ten square miles of virgin African bush, then an undeveloped farm in a pioneer district. Although wild game grazed peacefully everywhere, bounding away with an explosive snort or click of the heels when alarmed, my attention was invariably drawn to the flowers. I fell in love with them then and they have been my friends ever since.

One of my favourites was the Fireball Lilly *(Scadoxus multiflorus),* thrusting out of the short green grass after the rains had broken, like a gigantic pink shaving brush. It often nestled in a clump beneath a group of Acacia trees or stood up on the side of a six-foot-high anthill. Then there was *Gloriosa superba,* a magnificent lily with a brilliant flower fashioned with reflexed scarlet petals striped yellow and green. It climbed out of the tall grasses by means of delicate tendrils at the end of its upper leaves. Many years later I came to know of a delightful variant—pale lemon yellow, with an amethystine stripe which preferred more arid and rocky regions.

Sometimes I brushed against a ten-foot-high orchid *(Eulophia horsfallii),* a swamp dweller which speared itself out of the oozy acid soil with bronze-purple flowers bedecking more than three feet of the stalk. As I travelled further than the confines of the farm I began to realise what an immense heritage of flowering trees and herbs belongs to Kenya, stretching all the way from the high alpine zones to the coral wrag along the Indian Ocean shore. Giant lobelias, every species specially adapted to its own mountain region, grow from 7,000 to 13,000 feet (2,200 to 4,300 metres), each plant from 10 to 13 feet (3 to 4 metres) in height.

Surpassing them in majesty are the Giant Groundsels *(Dendrosenecio),* up to 30 feet in height, again specialised to their alpine environonment. Nestled alongside are members of the Gentian and Primrose families of northern Europe.

At every different altitude and ecological zone, flower friends beckon to me—the select *Delphinium macrocentron* with its turquoise or blue flowers and a marked "pixie cap". And if I am lucky, a white species, *D. leroyii,* which is rare but well worth looking for. From 10,000 feet (3,300 metres) to sea level, the great *Crotalaria* genus grows (members of the pea family), often with spiky yellow flowers like lupins which cluster either in a small patch or in great drifts brightening up the grassy woodland.

In the swampy areas of the higher grassland are patches of Red Hot Poker, with the nodding *Dierama pendulum,* a relative of the Wind Flower, not so far away. In the warmer, wetter grasslands grow *Gladiolus* spp., and the superior brilliant red *G. watsonioides* and the flowers of the many species of hibiscus, some yellow with maroon centres, others grey-mauve, purple, white or red.

I love the trees—the Nandi Flame *(Spathodea nilotica)* with its magnificent open chalice-like orange-red flowers, and the tall *Cordia*

africana growing up to 60 feet (20 metres), covered with a mass of soft papery-white open flowers with their velvety-brown contrasting calyx. At lower altitudes where it is drier and warmer is *Erythrina abyssinica,* the vivid cork bark tree covered with bright vermilion spikes of flowers often close by great drifts of sweetly-scented white flowering *Acacias.*

Perhaps a few miles along the road are yellow flowering *Cassias,* often lighting up the grey immensity of the bush before the rains break, dazzling viewers with their unbelievable golden colours.

We must not forget the plants of the semi-arid regions or the drier grasslands, like the *aloes* which create startling patches of orange in the landscape. The elephants love their succulent roots and leaves and flowers, which appear like tufts on the end of long stems, peering out of the dry bushland. The beautiful yellow and brown *Cistanche tubulosa* displays itself like a large hyacinth, leafless on the bare patches of red earth in the warmer, more arid areas, a parasite on the roots of neighbouring shrubs or trees. The *Ornitholgalums,* relatives of the Star of Bethlehem in northern climates, are also present, with their attractive cool-looking white and green flowers. Then there are orchids in the woodland and forest areas, in the deep recesses of river valleys and on remote mountain tops jutting out of the semi-desert regions from the Leopard orchid *(Ansellia gigantea)* among the palm trees of the coast to the delicate forest-loving *Polystachya spp.,* of the upland forests. We also see different species of *Ipomoea,* the *Convolvulus* or birdweed family of other continents, spreading along the sand at the coast, erect and trumpet-faced in the grasslands and scrambling or peeking out of the dark green riverine bush. And in the shadier moister places along streams or near waterfalls, we find the wonderful Balsams *(Impatiens),* pink, white or mauve-purple.

I regret only that it is possible to mention so few of the six thousand or more different species which beckon the visitor—flowers and bush, displaying themselves in the brazen African sunlight or pointing up to the cerulean sky out of the short tussocky grasses of the mountain areas. The traveller will find that discovering flowers and trees at every turn of a path, on the moorlands, in the wide plains, the rocky outcrops and lava belts, and in the warm coastal belt of this remarkable country, well rewards his journey.

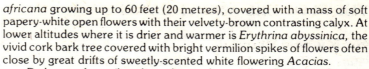

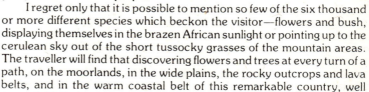

COASTAL SITES AND MONUMENTS

Omar Bwana

*Head of the coastal sites and monuments for the
National Museums of Kenya*

Fort Jesus

Visitors who flock to this country to see its spectacular game parks and palm-lined beaches are often completely unaware of a different attraction: the historical monuments and archaeological sites of the Kenya coast. There, ruined towns, a well preserved Portuguese fort and reconstructed villages reflect the rich cultural heritage of the region which has been visited by adventurers, conquerors, travellers and traders for several thousand years.

The National Museum's historic sites and monuments have been designed to provide the casual visitor with the greatest variety of experiences. Most are easily accessible to tourists, many of whom welcome a change from game viewing, ocean sports and sunbathing. Guidebooks, labelled displays and supplementary books are available on most sites for the serious visitor, while those who wish to relax can settle down with a picnic in the special areas reserved for holiday makers. Whatever tourists desire, they should take time to visit the magnificent historical museums and monuments of the beautiful Kenya coast.

The first stop for many visitors is Fort Jesus, the oldest fortress built by a European power in Africa. Overlooking Mombasa Harbour, Fort Jesus was built by the Portuguese in 1593, and changed hands violently many times before it came under the administration of the National Museums in 1969. Today it attracts more than 150,000 visitors each year. They come to view well preserved artifacts from coastal sites, relics from a Portuguese frigate sunk 300 years ago in the Mombasa harbour, and the "material culture" of Old Town Mombasa. Visiting the fort is a relaxing and interesting experience for visitors, most of whom finish their tour high up on the battlements where they can sip a glass of chilled lime juice while enjoying the sight of the beautiful Indian Ocean.

Fort Jesus gate

To be transported back to the 15th century visit Gedi, a 45-acre site a few kilometres from Malindi, where the ruins of the golden era of Islamic culture are preserved. Although a comprehensive guidebook unlocks some of the mysteries of Gedi, to this day no one knows why the apparently thriving town was abandoned early in the 17th century. What remains of the town does give us many clues to the lives of its inhabitants, however. Visitors can wander through the old streets, exploring the well preserved houses, several mosques (including a large "Friday Mosque") and study elaborate pillar tombs and a palace which covers a quarter of an acre. Inside the palace walls, the grand audience court remains, with a bench along the east end where judges sat, well protected from the midday sun. In the little museum, there are household utensils on exhibit, as well as Chinese porcelain bowls which indicate the town's extensive trade.

Gedi offers something for everyone: innumerable opportunities for photography, a pleasant place to picnic, a rich variety of bird and animal life, and an unforgettable introduction to early coastal architecture. Near the ruins the Giriama (coastal people of the area), have constructed a

Pillar tomb,
Gedi

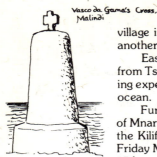
Vasco da Gama's Cross,
Malindi

village in their traditional fashion, giving visitors a chance to explore another aspect of contemporary coastal life.

Easily accessible from the marine parks at Malindi and Watamu, and from Tsavo Game Park, Gedi provides a relaxing interlude and stimulating experience for those who have been viewing animals or enjoying the ocean.

Further up the coast on the south bank of Kilifi Creek are the ruins of Mnarani, a national monument which is ideal to visit while waiting for the Kilifi Ferry. It's a short walk to the ruins, which comprise a large Friday Mosque, a smaller mosque and a group of tombs dating from the 15th century. The site is well known for the quality and quantity of the inscriptions and carvings which decorate the mosques and tombs. One of the finest pillar tombs on the coast is at Mnarani, where the design is unique. High above the blue-green waters of Kilifi Creek, Mnarani is a scenic, peaceful spot well worth a visit.

Carved door,
Lamu

On the north coast, the Lamu Archipelago is well known for gorgeous beaches, beautiful reefs and fine fishing. Lamu town is world famous for magnificent old houses, narrow streets, delicate wood carvings, numerous mosques and living Swahili culture. The Lamu Museum, one of the best small museums in Africa, shares this world renown. The exhibits on display represent the material culture of various coastal peoples in the context in which the items are used, such as rooms depicting a traditional Swahili wedding and coastal maritime culture. There is a very special exhibit of ivory and brass siwas, magnificent ceremonial musical instruments which were used, and still are, on special occasions in the town.

While visiting Lamu, take a traditional lateen-rigged dhow to the ruins of Takwa, a national monument on nearby Manda Island. Takwa is a 16th century site covering 12 acres, on which there are the remains of 150 coral structures, including a congregational mosque, an outstanding pillar tomb and many houses. There are huts available for anyone wishing to camp by the ruins. There they can enjoy moonlit walks along the beach, the rich flora and a wide variety of animals, ranging from dik-dik to elephants.

Gedi Palace

A WALK THROUGH OLD TOWN MOMBASA

Andrew Hall
Artist, and manager of Gallery Mash'a Allah

As you arrive in Mombasa for the first time, you get the impression of a fairly busy, reasonably modern port town, with traffic lights and round-abouts, street-side cafes and modern boutiques, high-rise buildings and the inevitable odour of diesel and petrol fumes.

Now take a drive down Nkrumah Road from the town centre towards Fort Jesus. You pass some old colonial buildings and modern office blocks, traffic signs and well dressed pedestrians. Pass through Treasury Square, which will remind you of a past colonial era with its arched and pillared architecture, down towards the water's edge at Tudor Creek. Suddenly you are in a different world entirely, away from the noise of traffic and the hum of air-conditioners into a world of narrow shaded streets of an age long gone.

This is the old town of Mombasa which retains its own pace and culture. You enter this world on a street called Ndia Kuu Road meaning "high street," which looks much as it did at the turn of the century when it was the hub of Mombasa, except now the camels have turned into cars and cows are not allowed to roam around at will. Of course the rain, humidity and heat have taken their toll on the old buildings, and the finely carved wooden balconies have lost their finer details to wood rot and mould. A bearded Arab gentleman struts proudly by in his long spotless white jelabia and neatly bound turban, hardly turning to notice the camera-toting tourists or bargain hunting shoppers. A veiled young lady in a long black *bui bui* (the traditional dress of Swahili women) sweeps by, leaving a trail of jasmine-scented air. One wonders what beauty that black veil may conceal.

Huge heavily carved doors, their immense chains and giant pad-locks made of solid brass, appear to support the tall houses. Antique buyers cast envious eyes upon the well-worn locks and tempt the owners with all kinds of combination padlocks and magnetic keys. They fail, and the huge brass locks hang there for yet another hundred years.

You suddenly become aware of time at the striking of an old railway pendulum clock, its deep hollow sound echoing from an even narrower dark steet. On entering the street, you find an open door and large nule post made of teak wood darkened by age. As your eyes adjust to the dim interior you can see the most magnificant stairway leading upward into darkness. To where or to what you may never know. Suddenly a shriek and squeal, as two fighting cats tumble down the stairs and into the bright street.

Continuing down Ndia Kuu you meet a kindly old man at a fruit stall, piled with green limes and neat rows of ripe oranges and mangoes. Baskets full of ripe red tomatoes lie there too, and a bowl of some dark purple fruit you have never seen before. The wise old fruit seller sees you staring at it and immediately removes one, polishes it up on his sarong, and hands it to you with a toothless smile. "Is this really edible?" He answers with a nod. It doesn't taste too bad after all, kind of sweet and sour together and somehow grapelike. It is called Zambarai, meaning

purple in Swahili; he says it grows in the jungle! Well who knows, let's just leave it a mystery.

Your attention is diverted by the clinking of small cups and along shuffles a coffee seller with a large cone-shaped brass coffeepot and masses of tiny china cups. He pours one, a sample cup which smells as strong as it tastes, spicy, black, strong and very bitter and, if that doesn't put some life into you, nothing will. He sees the look on your face, grins and shuffles on.

From a turret which rises high above the rusted iron roofs and pealing walls comes the backoning call of the muezzin. "Allah u Akbar, Allah u Akbar!" (" God is great"). Stores begin to close and the Muslims make their way to the mosque for midday prayers, washing their hands and feet before entering the mosque and facing Mecca.

Though the atmosphere is very Islamic, Mombasa still has large numbers of Hindu temples. The Jains have their ornate white temple situated on the old Kilindini Road. There are Catholics from Goa, Parsees from India and a great many more.

Suddenly you find yourself in the old port square where huge articulated trucks await cargo, unloaded from the Arab dhows by hand. Like a trail of ants, stevedores, doubled over with the weight, muscles bulging and bodies glistening with sweat, wind their way from the rocking ships up to the waiting trucks.

The dhow crews, a motley bunch of what appear to be *Arabian Nights* pirates with ragged turbans, dark sun-scorched faces and blackened teeth, stand aloof on the upper decks watch their cargos of cardamom, ginger, cloves, dried shark or masala powder being unloaded.

You leave this ancient scene to the sound of chanting, as sacks fall from the ship to the dock with clockwork efficiency. You wonder when the first crane will be installed and change this magic scene forever.

Walking along Mbarak Hinawy Road, formerly Vasco da Gama Street, toward Fort Jesus, you pass a 16th-century mosque, unchanged and still used, as is its old water well, for pre-prayer ablutions. The wooden overhanging balconies shade the hot street, and young girls and children peer below to see who passes. The mingled smell of fish and scents of jasmine and cooking spices drift lazily in the air as you return to the main Nkrumah Road and the twentieth century. An air-conditioned tourist bus and the power cables and transformers, the hawkers and the business people driving in for lunch at the Club confirm the present.

MOMBASA
TOWN CENTRE

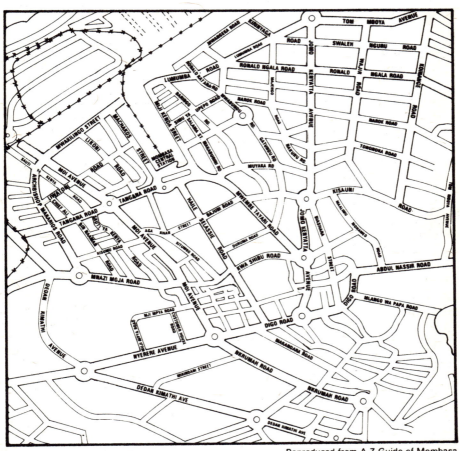

Reproduced from A-Z Guide of Mombasa
© Kenway Publications

THE ANCIENT ART OF BARGAINING

Mike Eldon

For anyone used to buying in supermarkets, the challenge of bargaining is often more forbidding than any other aspect of a safari. After all, it's a sport which few westerners have ever watched, much less participated in. And suddenly, here you are, your manhood (or womanhood) on the line, obligated to put on a show for both vendor and fellow tourists.

A mixture of emotions overcomes the novice trader. On the one hand, you don't wish to appear too aggressive. After all, the last thing you wish to be accused of is being a mean neocolonialist exploiter. On the other hand, the game is there to be played; and you can't afford to be labelled a 'chicken'!

But what is too tough and what is too lenient? If a shopkeeper asks for X, do you offer ten per cent less? One-tenth? How do you know? Where do you start? Regrettably (or enjoyably) there is no guideline. It's all to do with feelings, inner strength and, ultimately, with what you think the item is worth to you.

The first rule about bargaining is fundamental. You must learn to enjoy it. Some people are natural bargainers, while others only learn through experience—and some poor failures just can't seem to get away from the supermarket mentality. But unless you decide to have fun, you'll never be any good. Linked with this enjoyment is a warning against becoming too dedicated. Remember, it's a game, not a life-and-death contest of wills and ego.

The perfect finish to a session is when both parties feel they've won. Each side has given away more than it would have wished, but both participants feel there has been good sport and that the outcome was amicable: willing buyer, willing seller.

As with any sport, bargaining has its standard gambits, and it is very important to be familiar with the shots which keep the banter going. From the shopkeeper you will hear that he "can't possibly go any lower." He'll imploringly tell you that the price is already reduced; he bought it for more than you are offering; he only operates on fixed prices; the deal is special for you; the product is special for you; both... and so on.

For your part, you must show sympathy and understanding. And then counter with such old favourites as: shock and horror; regret; pseudo walk-out; actual walk-out (the final test); expressions of disinterest in the product; request for final 'best' price; offense that tourist prices are being charged.

Above all, be creative. Go beyond these regular ploys. Get an extra knick-knack thrown in, or seek a further discount if you buy more than one item. Work in teams—all the best negotiating combinations have a goodie and a baddie, with the goodie always ready to close the deal and the baddie holding him back. Try alternating the roles too and don't forget to play to the gallery. The opposition certainly will.

The real bargainer is the person who follows through with the apres-bargain banter, consoling the poor out-manoeuvred loser—all the time trying his damndest to persuade himself he really did strike a good deal. The match is over, it's time to relax—and snitch an extra final discount?

LIVE YOUR SAFARI MOMENT BY MOMENT

Mary Anne Fitzgerald

A freelance journalist who has made Kenya her base while covering East Africa for the Christian Science Monitor, London Sunday Times *and* The Economist

In northern Kenya young warriors from the Samburu tribe wear bright, beaded bracelets in the shape of a watch. There is something to be learned from this irreverent comment on the Western preoccupation with timekeeping. Africa moves at a slow and gentle pace. If you want to enjoy your safari to the hilt, the first thing to do is to fall in with its leisurely pace. After all, you are on holiday now.

There are no appointments to keep except, possibly, lunch or dinner. Slow down. Look around you and savour the singular smells, sights and colours. Leave time on your itinerary to explore the unexpected when it happens. It may be a porcupine crossing the road that deposits a perfectly fashioned black and white quill in the dust as a parting present. Pick it up. Or a breathtaking view of volcanic mountains shimmering in the noonday sun. Pull over and take a photo. Or a roadside stall selling fresh plums or sheepskin hats. Stop to investigate.

Making the purchase is only half the experience. The other half is the friendly chat that Kenyans enjoy so much. It will elicit whose orchard the fruit came from or how the hat was made. A friendship has been struck and a moment translated into a memory.

Visitors are all too often shepherded around from lodge to hotel with the countryside flowing past in a kaleidoscopic vision of changing scenery. This is not the place for the "if it's Tuesday it must be Keekorok" syndrome. Readjust your inner clock to a more tranquil lifestyle.

Dawn comes suddenly in Kenya. It is always a spectacular event. The sun breaks out of an eggshell sky and brushes the plains with Tintoretto blues and pinks. All too often visitors miss this rewarding part of the day, but they shouldn't.

In the city the rush hour has already begun as hundreds of workers stream down the road to offices and factories. In the country children are running barefoot to wooden school houses and lions pad softly down riverbeds in search of a meal.

In a land where much of the rural population has no access to electricity, life is synchronised to the sun. Activity for man and beast is at its height during the early hours and in the brief cool of the late afternoon. For, by nine o'clock, be it game park or beach, you will already be bathed in sweat and, until you get used to them, you'll be brushing aside swarms of flies.

Later on in the day there will be plenty of time for a siesta. The animals retire into the shade; you might as well follow suit.

Nights are imbued with equal promise. When the rest of the world has retired, there is nothing quite like being alone with the crickets and rustling palms painted by a silver moon. A lion's roar, instead of that of a car, is a happy reminder of our own small part in the grand cosmic order. Silence is a rare commodity in today's world. Take advantage of that too.

Many visitors view their safari as some sort of pleasurable endu-

rance test highlighted by glimpses of stunning scenery, colourful people and herds of wild animals. Again, take the time to enjoy it. If you visit the game parks with a worthwhile guide, he will know how to do it.

Many are of the belief that success is rated by the number of animals ticked off on an imaginary or real check list in the shortest possible time. That's no way to tackle the unprecedented opportunities for wildlife viewing that will present themselves. Instead, indulge in some of the recommended reading on wildlife mentioned in this guide. This will help you to identify the smaller creatures and the birds. Then, if something strikes your fancy, spend half an hour observing it and become acquainted with its habits and characteristics firsthand.

Tell your guide you are not in a hurry despite the watch you wear. A lion crouched in the grass, tail switching and eyes scanning the horizon, is a signal that he is looking for supper. Stop the car and wait. Before the hour is up you may very well have witnessed the unparalleled spectacle of a lioness bringing down a gazelle in full flight.

As you travel it is also rewarding to make the acquaintance of locals, many of whom speak good English. Kenyans are exceptionally friendly people who have a tradition of oral communication. They delight in explaining the history, customs and geography of their home. Seen through their eyes, a superficially stark landscape unfolds into a rich tapestry of intricate social customs and intriguing natural history.

In the more remote areas there is virtually no public transport, but this does not deter anyone from embarking on a fifty-mile trip on foot. There are no exceptions. Even the blind stride out alongside a friend, guided by the sound of his footsteps. When asked the objective of a journey the customary reply is, "To see my brother." These hikers, when encountered on the road, are delighted to be given a lift.

Should destinations differ, a drink of water is a welcome gesture of friendship that can lead to a photographic session that otherwise would be out-of-bounds, as most people tend to be camera shy.

Village tea shops also lend entertaining insights into community life just as boulevard cafes do in Europe. Even though they conform to the description of "fly-blown" and "dirty", do not be deterred. The customary fare is a tin mug of sweet, milky tea and a plate of *mandazis*, triangular cakes that taste like unsweetened doughnuts.

In order to enjoy these small delights, don't be overambitious when planning your itinerary. Some tour companies tend to draw up schedules that make the Paris-Dakar Rally pale by comparison. Maps can be misleading when organising safaris. Disregard distances and seek local advice as to how many hours the journey will take.

In some places the roads no longer resemble standard highways and can pose a challenge to both man and machine. It is not unknown to take a whole day to drive fifty miles. Visitors should plan to spend most of their time at their destinations—not trying to get there.

So bear in mind the Samburu warriors who tell the time by the sun. Perhaps you should pack away your watch and try it yourself. It is a noteworthy fact that despite their high cholesterol diet of milk and meat, the Samburu are never treated for high blood pressure.

HOW TO SURVIVE A SAFARI ... AND STILL LOOK GREAT!

Clare Maxwell-Hudson

Beauty therapist and author of The Natural Beauty Book *and*
Your Health and Beauty Book

After nine hours of bouncing around in a Land-Rover, most of us emerge looking—and feeling—thoroughly bedraggled. Our clothes are crushed, our faces are filthy, our lips are cracked and our hair is matted. But, occasionally, you see someone who looks as though she stepped off the front page of *Vogue* rather than the all-night bus from Mombasa. How does she do it?

Starting at the top—with the hair. If you are lucky, yours is either very short, or long enough to put up and out of the way. Even so, wisps have an infuriating habit of escaping, so the best solution is to cover it all up with a scarf. Use a cotton scarf (silk and synthetics are hopeless as they always slip off) or wear a comfortable, squashable hat which will not only protect your hair, but will also protect your skin from the sun.

Speaking of skin, if possible, don't wear any makeup, as the heat which builds up beneath your foundation will block your pores. Make-up usually goes streaky—and mascara often ends up everywhere but on your lashes. To avoid this, have your eyelashes dyed before you come. They'll last for three to four weeks, and the job can be done at any beauty salon.

Travelling is a hot, dusty business, and it is hard to feel glamorous with a sweaty face. To combat this, remember to take a cucumber... and a penknife, along on safari. When you are feeling hot and sticky, simply take a slice of the cucumber and wipe your face with it. This is not only wonderfully refreshing, but it's also a beauty treatment in itself, as the pH of the skin and the cucumber is the same—making the cucumber a perfect skin tonic. If your eyes are tired, soothe them with a slice of cucumber. And when you are feeling thirsty you can quench your thirst (and your appetite) by taking a large bite of your juicy cucumber!

When you arrive at your lodge or hotel, you'll probably be longing to scrub away all the accumulated dirt of the day. Use your own home-made face scrub, which works just as well as the new exfoliating creams and washes on the market. You will need to mix together 1/3 cup fine oatmeal, 1/3 cup gram flour and enough honey and water to make a thick paste. Stir a little with a dry finger (never put a wet finger into the jar, or the mixture will go "off") and put a small amount into the palm of the other hand, mix with water and wash with it. The oatmeal is abrasive, and the gram flour is a wonderful cleanser (much less drying than soap), while the honey is a natural moisturizer.

You can wash with gram flour alone which is very good, but not as abrasive as the mixture. Both methods leave the skin feeling wonderfully smooth and clean.

When you are at the coast, scrub yourself with seaweed. The iodine it contains has a stimulating effect on the skin, and is thought to be very effective in the battle against cellulite. If you feel your thighs could be improved, scrub them with seaweed every day.

On safari you will need to take a rich face cream to counteract the drying effects of the sun and dust, as well as a body lotion or almond oil to smooth and soothe the skin. Keep the oil in a plastic bottle to avoid disastrous breakages in your suitcase. Incidentally, once you have a slight tan, you can mix almond oil with vinegar and tea to make a mild suntan cream. The tea acts as a sunblock while the vinegar prevents burning and keeps insects away.

If, despite your efforts, the heat has made you react with spots, calm them down with a yoghurt mask. Simply apply a thin layer of plain yoghurt to the face and leave it on for ten minutes before rinsing it off. Yoghurt has an almost miraculous effect on the skin, and even severe cases of acne can be cured by this simple remedy applied each day. If yoghurt isn't available in the bush, maybe you can find a slice of tomato. The tomato juice is acidic and will dry up spots very quickly.

For dry or sunburned skin apply a pawpaw mask. Pawpaws have traditionally been used in Kenya to heal wounds and tenderize meat. They have the same effect on the face, leaving the skin smooth and soft.

Give dry and dehydrated skin an avocado face mask. The oil from the avocado is the most similar to the skin's natural oil and therefore mashed avocados make a wonderfully rejuvenating mask. To make any of these fruit masks use about a tablespoon of the flesh, mash it up and apply to the skin. Leave it on for about 10 minutes before rinsing off.

If you go on safari with a few basic items in your travel bag, you should be able to return home looking as good—if not better—than when you began!

Happy Safari!

Survival Kit for Safaris
cotton scarf or comfortable hat
sunblock
suntan lotion or cream
cleansing cream
rich face cream
body lotion or almond oil

Bush Alternatives
oatmeal
gram flour
honey
cucumber
yoghurt
tomato juice
pawpaw
avocados

A CONNOISSEUR'S GUIDE TO SHOPPING

Kathy Eldon

A sense of desperation seems to overcome newly arrived tourists in Kenya. As if terrified that the shops will disappear before they have a chance to buy, they tear out of their hotels, racing towards the City Market with its alluring merchandise and colourful characters.

There really is no rush; with at least two weeks before the average visitor, there is plenty of time to look around, to gauge what is for sale and what's worth buying. Items which appeal at the beginning of the trip may look like tourist junk by the end of the safari. To avoid costly errors, take your time.

The devaluation of the Kenya shilling and the increasing strength of western currencies, means there are more bargains to be found every year, usually hand-crafted items fashioned from local materials. Most accessible to the tourist are wood carvings, which abound on every street corner. They come in two varieties: the first is the category of mass-produced curios, hand-carved by craftsmen working to a set formula. Animals, salad bowls and servers, book-ends, napkin rings, bracelets and belt buckles are usually good buys, particularly when you remember that once you have taken them home to Cleveland, Frankfurt or Rome, no one else will have anything like them on the mantlepiece.

The second category of wooden carvings includes the "one-of-a-kind" pieces, genuine works of art carved by individual craftsmen working from their own inspiration. Watch out for Makonde carvings, fashioned in heavy black ebony, usually by Tanzanian carvers. Sometimes highly erotic, they can be elegantly abstract in their design, or a swirling mass of humanity, as in the "Ujamaa" pieces, which represent the Tanzanian socialist philosophy of "working together".

Brass-trimmed carved coastal furniture, mirrors, boxes, candle-holders and bracelets illustrate the Swahili love of decoration. Examine the carving carefully and avoid those which have been crudely executed. Antique carvings are around, though difficult to find—and expensive.

Kisii soapstone carvings provide an alternative to those made of wood. Although the larger pieces are terribly heavy (though wonderfully sensuous), smaller articles such as candleholders, sugar pots, vases, animals and birds, can be carefully wrapped and tucked into odd corners of the suitcase. Remember that soapstone is brittle and cracks easily, so decorative items are likely to last longer than functional pieces.

Sisal animals, place mats and wall hangings are light, easy to transport souvenirs which will appeal to the folks back home. Look for finely woven items, well-finished with all the ends trimmed and tucked away. By far the most popular of all sisal products are "kiondos", otherwise known as "Kenya bags". Currently, Kenya exports more than 200,000 bags every month, each one painstakingly woven by women, usually members of co-operative organisations which provides them with an outlet for their bags, and a desperately needed income. Natural earth tones denote traditional kiondos, while the brilliantly coloured bags are the new rage overseas. Check the handles before buying and look for well-crafted, sturdy leather straps which will last just as long as the bag... that is, forever!

Jewellers shops display tempting Kenyan semi-precious stones made into attractive, if expensive clocks, vases, eggs and cutlery handles. Bargain vigorously, as prices are set for the gullible. A few gemstones are good buys, especially tanzanite, discovered in 1967 in Tanzania. It is a crystal form of zoizite and ranges in colour from intense blue to a lilac hue. Tanzanite has a hardness rating of 6½ (which is fairly soft) and possesses the quality of "dichroism" which means it changes its colour when viewed along different axes. Named by Tiffany's, the stone has become world famous and is expected to appreciate significantly in value. The same is true of tsavorite, a vivid green garnet discovered near Tsavo National Park in 1973 by prospectors from Eltons Jewellers in Nairobi. Harder and more durable than emerald, it may one day overtake emeralds in value. Before purchasing any gemstone, examine it carefully beneath a magnifying glass to reveal any flaws or irregular cutting.

Cheap and cheerful batiks are everywhere. Costing less than 200/-, they will look great once framed and hung in the hallway at home, but for collector's batiks, visit art galleries and expect much higher prices. The same is true of "fun" jewellery. Buy pounded brass, cheaply-made Maasai necklaces and bracelets on the street, but don't expect high quality. That costs money, both for the original designs and for the more costly materials like amber, old Ethiopian silver beads and colourful trade beads.

Anyone who doesn't know what to buy should have a look at the colourful and inexpensive Kenyan fabrics. Traditionally worn by women, printed pieces of material called *kangas* and *kitenges* are perfect for wall hangings, tablecloths, beach wraps and bedspreads. Woven, striped *kikois*, formerly reserved as the garb of coastal men, and now often fashioned into shirts and dresses, can be used instead of pajamas as the perfect garb for bedtime wear.

kikoi   kanga

A walk down Nairobi's Biashara Street or through Mombasa's market area will reveal shops filled with open bags of exotic spices. Pre-mixed "masalas", combinations of spices suitable for curries or sweet tea, make excellent little gifts, as do tiny carved animals, Kenya-inspired stationery, carved combs, old headrests and copper jewellery (the raw materials of which are often telephone wires).

When in doubt, buy what you like and worry about the money when the credit card bill arrives!

CARVINGS GENUINE EBONY

BEYOND THE CURIOS

Kamal Shah
Artist, craftsman and creative director of Rowland Ward Gallery in Nairobi

An explosion is taking place on the Nairobi art scene. The city is alive with numerous exhibitions and shows. This, together with a more interested media covering the events, makes for a productive and inspiring atmosphere for artists as well as their audiences.

Apart from the more established showplaces like the Gallery Watatu, African Heritage and Rowland Ward Gallery, cultural centres of France, Germany, the United States, Italy and Britain have been active in promoting Kenyan artists. There are also occasional shows at City Hall and the Kenyatta Conference Centre, some sponsored by the Ministry of Culture and Social Services, which is increasingly active in promoting the arts.

There are a few colourful personalities among local artists who shine above the others. The undisputed father of the modern art movement in Kenya is Ancien Soi, a self-taught artist who has painted consistently for more than two decades. He has won many international awards, including the honour of having one of his paintings selected as the Olympic Games poster in 1972. His works feature in the prestigious Commonwealth Institute in London and the Council House collection in the States. His vividly colourful and detailed large-scale canvases portray varied themes: tribal images, energetic wildlife in idyllic tropical landscapes, contemporary Nairobi cityscapes as well as Bible stories. His paintings are unique commentaries on both traditional culture and modern city life.

Whimsical, lyrical, magical, softly surreal, personal and very Freudian are all terms which have been used to describe the works of Jak Katarikawe. Influenced as a young man by the Makerere School in Uganda, Jak's soft pastel-toned paintings tell of astounding fantasies intermingled with folklore, animal and personal mythologies. His animal paintings, especially those with cow themes, are heavily sensuous, a feeling made disconcerting by the nearly human eyes and expressions of the cows. Jak is one of the only artists in Nairobi who does not "moonlight" at other jobs.

Serious sculptors are few and far between. In a city where curio carvings are much in demand, not many carvers are willing to venture into unknown territory. However, there are some notable exceptions: one is Samuel Wanjau, whose large wooden sculptures of surreal insects and people have received critical acclaim at home and abroad.

Michael Dimo's powerful wooden heads and grotesques are among the most original sculptures found in Nairobi. He makes excellent use of the grain found in exotic woods, resulting in aggressive sculpture which attracts a devoted, if limited, following.

Sculptor Expedito Mwebe has diversified from sculptures to fanciful carvings which decorate many buildings in Nairobi, including the Lillian Towers swimming pool complex and the Meridian Court Hotel entrance. Expedito has created a series of finely designed combs and other articles

of practical use.

In an effort to foil the "copy cats" who have imitated his original banana fibre creations, craftsman Stephen Munga has recently made a dramatic debut as a mask maker. His awesome masks are made from a variety of materials and are contemporary works which reflect the aesthetic sense of their maker.

Gourd incising is a traditional craft brought up-to-date by Peter Nzuki, whose fine lyrical line is most distinctive. Equally delicate are the clay busts modelled by Henry Dullo, whose observant eye parallels that of painter Katarikawe: he captures each physical and psychological characteristic of his sitter.

The futility of trying to categorise individuals under the label, "artist" or "craftsman" is made obvious when one sees the bicycle paintings of Mpata and Elizabeth, a husband-and-wife team who create their bright naive paintings on hardboard with gloss paint. The style was developed by Mpata in Tanzania where many artists now work in a similar style, often decorating functional items to brighten the homes of ordinary people.

Part time artists abound in Nairobi: John Githinji delights gallery-goers with his biting cartoons, while Sukuro's large mural paintings continue to impress. Sav Boro and Martin Ngatia follow in the footsteps of their mentor Keith Harrington, the unsurpassable landscape painter. Daniel Njoroge is beginning to excel in his photo-realistic style producing renditions of tribal lifestyles in watercolour and oils, and Mary Collis has expanded her techniques into light-filled abstract paintings. Moyra Owens' incisive wit permeates her satirical cartoons, while batik-makers Sekanwagi and Nnyanzi battle to give their medium a better image.

Wildlife painters such as Robert O'Meara, Thuo Kiragu, William Baker and Jonathon Scott produce sought-after and very professional paintings, while the flamboyant works of Joni Waite and Theresa Musoke reflect their irrepressible and exuberant spirits. Nani Croze's staind glass works provide a new insight into this prolific artist, who works in a sun-filled studio on the Athi Plains, while Heidi Lange remains an inspiring and prolific designer, producing some of Kenya's most appealing (and unscrupulously copied) batik prints. The new Gallery Tazama provides a dramatic view of Robin Anderson's splendid silk-screened batik prints, each one framed and spotlit on rough white walls.

With such a plethora of choices, visitors should have little difficulty in finding a unique treasure to take home as a reminder of Kenya.

STRETCHING YOUR CAMERA

Advice compiled by Mike Eldon with the technical assistance of the Camera Maintenance Centre, Hilton Hotel

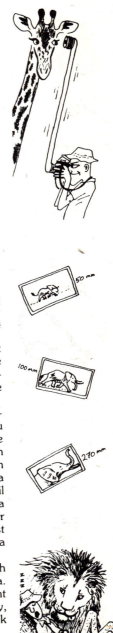

How many boxes of old slides clutter your attic? How many piles of envelopes full of unsorted prints? And, more to the point, will your safari pictures simply join this forgotten archive, gathering dust for posterity?

Surely it would be a shame if the excitement of an African hunting expedition simply fizzled out shortly after you return home: the final thrill of seeing the developed product and then... oblivion.

Give some thought, therefore, before the trigger-happy momentum allows you to get carried away, as to what you would like to achieve of more lasting value. And bear in mind that for most safari-snappers, photography is limited to a compulsive, semi-mindless consumption of film which distracts them from really enjoying the experience itself and gives them limited pleasure thereafter.

Aim at producing a few real masterpieces to enlarge and frame; if you are taking prints, visualise their layout and presentation in an album; for slides, start evolving the structure and script for a show which will be both informative and aesthetically pleasing; select some themes which you can develop. In these and other ways, the popping of individual shots is transformed into a purposeful exercise, stretching your creative talents, and forcing you to greater understanding of the setting within which your photography is taking place.

Many people are insecure about what camera to take, and feel that they could only cope with an "autofocus" and normal 50 mm lens. These new cameras, with their ease of operation and built-in flashes, are wonderful for general photography. However, if you are thinking of game photography, then a telephoto lens is essential.

The best choice is a single-reflex lens camera with a through-the-lens light-meter. Cameras normally are sold with a 50mm lens, and you can either take along a fixed-focus or a zoom telephoto lens. Some experts recommend the purchase of a 135 mm lens and a doubler, which gives the photographer a choice of 50mm, 100mm, 135mm or 270mm with a minimum of extra equipment. Zoom lenses give different and extra flexibility: having fixed the light and focus, you can zoom in and out until the picture is perfectly framed. A doubler is not recommended on a zoom lens, as the light is not sufficient. Fit all lenses with an ultra-violet or skylight filter in order to protect them from scratches or dust, and invest in a device which attaches the lens cap to the camera. When the camera is not in use, wrap it in a towel to protect it from vibration and dust.

Before setting out on safari, you should try to become familiar with the loading, unloading, speed, light and focus-settings of the camera. Experiment by taking the same view at different settings for different effects; play with the different lenses, learn how to change them quickly, and utilise the zoom. Above all, learn to relax with the camera and look for interesting or original compositions.

Film is expensive in Kenya, particularly in lodges, so be sure to buy all you need before going on safari. The average photographer takes at least 600 stills, though enthusiasts have been known to take double or three

times that amount during a two-week safari. Most professionals prefer 100 ASA for prints and 200 ASA for slides, with 400 ASA film for early mornings or dusk when the light is dim.

Now to photographing the animals themselves. If you are anything like the average tourist, then the moment your vehicle enters the game park for the first time, you will succumb to the temptation of shooting anything that moves. Don't! Take it easy, absorb the atmosphere and talk to your driver. He'll size you up very quickly and give excellent advice as to how to approach the shooting business. He'll find the animals, and will know how to approach them to allow you to get the best possible picture, from the best angle and in the best light. He'll also have a feel for whether you are just spotting for statistics, or whether you are more interested and patient enough to watch situations develop. Maybe the cheetah will yawn, the zebra foal with suckle, or the lioness will play with her cubs. But if they are too far away to see clearly, don't bother to take a picture, just enjoy the sight.

Cheetah Hunting

Patience is a virtue in photography—but so is speed of reaction. Have your camera ready with the most logical lens set at the most likely light setting... and film loaded. This way you won't risk cursing yourself for missing the greatest shot that would have been. Don't hesitate to ask the driver to stop suddenly—he will be pleased by the interest you are showing—but do gauge the patience of your fellow passengers. And on no account overestimate the tameness of the animals and try to leave the vehicle. It is also considered poor etiquette to provoke or disturb the animals.

The best time to catch the wildlife is at either end of the day when they are active or in the morning when the light is less harsh and more interesting. Do risk a few daring shots—sunsets, views into the light, a ridiculously close-up shot of a head. If they succeed you'll hit the jackpot.

Also try to provide the animals with an attractive background. This may be foliage, hills, sky or any other setting. Such compositions often lead to contrasts in lighting which are particularly tricky, and require a compromise setting to avoid over- or under-exposure of the subject.

More ambitious photographers can try shooting birds, but make sure your telephoto lens is powerful enough and expect to be very patient and very quiet. Bird photography is highly specialised and few tourists can manage much more than vultures over carcasses. But if the opportunity arises to capture a bird perched on a branch, the effect can be most artistic.

Finally, everyone would like to take home pictures of local people, and the Maasai in their full regalia are most tempting. A word of warning: most Kenyans are not at all keen to be photographed, so you should always politely ask permission before aiming. Some people are against posing in principle, others can be persuaded with a fee. For the latter, only you can decide how much the picture is worth—maybe buying a beaded necklace can be part of the deal, and part of a more enjoyable transaction.

With a little thought and a little luck, your camera can bring you enormous satisfaction on safari. Make the most of it and be sure of something beautiful and lasting to take back home.

THE KANGA STRUTS IN STYLE

Jeannette Hanby
Author of Kangas: 101 Uses

The sight of colourful kangas flapping in the breeze is common throughout East Africa. This simple rectangle of fabric is one of the most useful pieces of material ever invented. It is called a kanga in Kenya, though elsewhere in the tropics it has other names, such as "dhotie" or "sarong". Men sleep in kangas, and often wear them around the house; women wear them everywhere; babies are virtually born into them and spend their first year or so carried snugly in a soft sling of kanga cloth. Kangas are extremely popular throughout East Africa. They make an attractive gift with multiple uses; no one can ever have too many!

The kanga is a rectangle of pure cotton cloth with a border all around it, usually printed in bold designs and bright colours. It is as long as your outstretched arm and is wide enough to cover you from neck to knee, or from breast to toe.

Husbands give kangas to wives, children to their mothers; women may split a pair to give one half to their best friend. Tourists have discovered they make perfect gifts; unbreakable, light and inexpensive, they are welcomed by just about anyone. they make wonderful wall hangings, colourful tableclothes and ideal beach wraps for either sex. A few stitches turns a kanga into a cushion cover or a cool shirt or dress. The only problem facing the purchaser is the difficult decision of which kanga not to buy.

Kangas originated on the coast of East Africa in the mid-19th century. As the story goes, some stylish ladies in Zanzibar got the idea of buying printed kerchiefs in lengths of six from the bolt of cloth from which the kerchiefs were usually cut off and sold singly. They then cut the six into lengths of three and sewed these together to make a three-by-two sheet. Sometimes they bought different kinds of kerchiefs and sewed them back together to form very individualistic designs.

The new style was called "leso" after the kerchief squares which had originally been brought to Africa by Portuguese traders. The leso quickly became more popular than the other kind of patterned cloth available. Before long, enterprising coastal shopkeepers sent away for special designs, printed like the six-together leso pieces but as a single unit of cloth.

These early designs probably had a border and a pattern of white spots on a dark background. The buyers (or more likely, their menfolk) quickly came to call these cloths "kanga" after the noisy sociable guinea fowl with its elegant spotty plummage.

Kanga designs have evolved over the years, from simple spots and borders to a huge variety of elaborate patterns of every conceivable motif and colour. For a century, kangas were mostly designed and printed in India, the Far East and Europe. Even today, you will see old kangas that were printed in China or Japan. But since the 1950's, an increasing number of kangas have been designed and printed in Tanzania, Kenya and other African countries.

Early this century, Swahili sayings were added to kangas. Supposedly

this fashion was started by Kaderdina Hajee Essak, a locally famous trader in Mombasa. Known as "Abdulla", the trader created unique kangas distinguished by the mark "K.H.E. -Mali ya Abdulla" and discovered his kangas sold even better with the addition of a proverb. At first the sayings were printed in Arabic script, later in Roman letters. Many of them have the added charm of being obscure or ambiguous in their meaning. Even today, if you find a motto you can't figure out, ask several different Swahili speakers. You will get an equal number of different explanations!

New kanga designs appear every week, reflecting the very latest fashion. Some are simple, other highly intricate or abstract. Kangas can feature homey themes such as chickens, maize cobs or babies, or can depict famous attractions; mountains, monuments and wildlife. the conoisseur will detect noticeable regional differences. For example, most of the kangas decorated with mottoes are made in Kenya, while those commemorating social or political events are more commonly found in Tanzania.

The kanga is still evolving. Like the tee shirt, it is a valuable medium for personal, political, social and religious expression. As an art form as well as a beautiful and useful garment, the kanga has become an integral part of East African culture. As the saying goes, "the kanga struts in style. . .". Wear it with a smile!

THE FOOD OF CULTURES — A POTPOURRI

Kathy Eldon

The very first visitor to record his impressions of Kenya was an anonymous Greek seaman who wrote an account of his adventures along the coast in a pilot's book entitled *The Periplus of the Erythrean Sea* in AD 110. Unfortunately, he didn't describe the cuisine along the way, though he must have appreciated having a chance to replenish his supply of water and fresh food after the rigours of the open sea.

The Arabs arrived in the tenth century, the first people to bring along their own food. They sailed in with a supply of their favourite dried fruits, rice and spices, which they introduced to coastal settlements. The newcomers cheerfully married the locals, creating what has come to be known as the Swahili people. All along the coast, the Swahili culture survives, with their own delicious foods which represent a blend of African, Indian and Arab influences. Contemporary visitors must try coconut-flavoured curries, saffron-tinged rice, fish masalas, spiced tea, thick black coffee and syrupy cardamom-tinged sweets, all served with traditional coastal hospitality.

The Swahili way of life didn't travel inland, however, which meant the indigenous peoples subsisted on a diet heavy in sorghum and millet, supplemented by whatever fruits, roots and seeds they could find. The arrival of the Portuguese in 1496 changed all that, as adventurers and explorers introduced new foods from newly discovered lands. Thus Muscovy Duck, maize and bananas, pineapple, chillies, peppers, tobacco, sweet potatoes and manioc all arrived in East Africa. The Portuguese also brought oranges, lemons and limes from China and India and introduced domestic pigs and dogs. Much of what is now considered to be "traditional" African food was first introduced by the Portuguese, world travellers who appear to have been evangelistic in their attempts to spread Portuguese tastes around the world.

The British were the next great influence in Kenya, bringing with them new breeds of sheep, goats and cattle, as well as what they considered to be essential fruits and vegetables, like strawberries and artichokes! They introduced high quality coffee bushes from other parts of Africa, and taught their cooks how to make apple pie and lumpy custard, as well as which direction to pass the port. The British also imported 30,000 Indians to Kenya to build the great railway. At the turn of the century, when the railway was finally finished, thousands stayed on, many becoming cooks for British families. The Indian cooks transformed British habits, making curry, chapatis and chutney as much a part of Sunday lunch as roast beef had been in Yorkshire.

The twentieth century has brought many new influences to Kenya as new settlers, soldiers and tourists have passed through the country—some staying for a few weeks, and others lingering on for years. Now visitors can enjoy the cuisine of many nations prepared by Kenyan chefs using local ingredients. Kenyan waiters can instruct uncertain diners on the finer points of using chopsticks, or prepare flambe dishes to order in restaurants which wouldn't look out of place in London, Paris or New York.

Safari cooking amazes newcomers, who can scarcely believe the superb cuisine prepared in a rough camp kitchen. Although it may seem bizarre, the day begins with early morning tea served in the middle of absolutely nowhere. Following a rugged game drive, breakfast is served, usually a hearty Continental affair, complete with all the prerequisites such as eggs and bacon, sausage, toast and vintage marmalade.

The meal is the product of enormous skill: conditions in the bush are about as basic as they can possibly be. The safari cooks (or *mpishis*) bake bread in an old tin trunk over smouldering ashes, and somehow manage to prepare grand feasts over a smoky wood fire in the dim light of a paraffin lamp or two. Food is kept cold in gas fridges while perishable meats like chicken and mutton often arrive in camp "on the hoof", making their presence known by plaintive clucks and bleats.

Curiously enough, the only foods that are difficult for tourists to find are traditional Kenyan dishes. But in the last few years, a few hoteliers and restaurateurs have discovered that many visitors would like to try local foods, but lack the courage to venture away from well travelled tourist haunts. Now, some regional dishes are finding their way on to fancy menus though the best food is naturally found in private homes.

Adventurous types should wander along Mombasa's backstreets after dark when stalls appear from nowhere, with their owners selling chapati mayai, hot bhajias and freshly fried cassava crisps. Nairobi's central areas are deserted at night, but in the fringes of town the crowds gather, lured perhaps by the smell of seekh kebabs, and mushkaki barbecued in the open air. Kariokor Market at lunchtime is the place to find "nyama choma", roast meat cooked over charcoal and served without knives or forks on long wooden tables. The accompaniments are traditional too: sukuma wiki (greens with tomatoes and onions), irio, (a lovely pale green mixture of mashed peas, potatoes and maize), and little plates of chopped chillies and tomatoes. No meal is complete without ugali, a stiff maize porridge which owes its presence to the intrepid Portuguese explorers.

Upmarket diners can try smoked tuna fish, Kenyan-style lobsters and crayfish, superb steaks, Molo lamb and Bahati ducks in fine restaurants. They can spend a fortune on imported wines, or sample the best of Kenya's beers. Kenyan cheeses range from delicate Brie, rich Camemberts, herb flavoured cream cheeses and earthy blues, to hard Emmenthal, creamy cheddars and caraway cheese. Coffee is always freshly brewed from roast beans so highly prized on the world market. And Kenya Gold liqueur provides a treat to be remembered—it's an award winning coffee liqueur which ranks with the best found anywhere.

Sampling the myriad tastes of Kenya can provide full time entertainment for visitors to this land of contrasts, a country where many cultures live together in gastronomic harmony.

SOMETHING FOR THE COFFEE TABLE

Mike Eldon

As far as Kenya is concerned, the Africana book-cup runneth over. In the past few years, a plethora of beautiful books has appeared, covering every aspect of the country's past, present and future. Bookshops abound in Nairobi and Mombasa, offering much lower prices than those found in hotel and lodge shops.

Take time to browse in the bookshops, savouring the colourful covers such as that on the masterpiece *Maasai*, produced by American photographer Carol Beckwith and writer Ole Saitoti, an American-educated Maasai who translates the traditions and customs of his peoples for westerners.

Kenya's best known and most prolific photographer is Mohamed Amin, who together with Duncan Willetts and Brian Tetley has produced the beautiful *Journey through Kenya*. Like David Keith Jones' *Faces of Kenya* and Gerald Cubitt and Eva Robins' *The Book of Kenya*, it vividly portrays the people and animals of Kenya, as well as the dramatic and varied country in which they live. Amin has also produced *Cradle of Mankind*, a pictorial survey of Lake Turkana which resulted from driving around its inhospitable shores.

Safari, the East African Diary of a Photographer by Gunter Ziester and *On Safari in Kenya*, a pictorial guide to the parks and reserves by Michael Gore, provide very personal views of Kenya as does John Schmid's new book, *The Magic of Kenya*.

Other educational books concentrate on various aspects of game. *Pyramids of Life* by John Reader and Harvey Croze, is essential reading prior to visiting a game park. It explains how animals co-exist within their ecological system and shows how natural laws are obeyed. Esmond and Chryssee Bradley Martin have focused on one animal in *Run, Rhino, Run*. Illustrated with pictures by the ubiquitous Amin, it describes the plight of the rhino and the uses to which the unfortunate animal's horn is placed. *Among the Elephants* is Iain and Oria Douglas-Hamilton's account of their adventures in studying the lives of these highly social animals, while the newly published *Cheetah* is an account of another couple, Katherine and Karl Amman, whose remarkable photographs provide an insight into that elusive animal. *Portraits in the Wild*, a classic study of animals by Cynthia Moss, is a thoughtful study of nearly all the animals encountered on safari.

Ian Parker wrote *Ivory Crisis* in anger. In it, he analyses the work of the various gurus of conservation and systematically demolishes their philosophies. Less controversially, John Karmali's *Birds of Africa* is a must for bird lovers, who will also find John Williams *Field Guide to the National Parks of East Africa* and P.L. Britton's comprehensive *Birds of East Africa* good companions. Sir Michael Blundell's *Wild Flowers of Kenya* and *African Blossoms* by Dorothy and Bob Hargreaves should be in every safari vehicle, along with Michael Tomkinson's popular *Kenya—a Holiday Guide*, a chatty and informative handbook. The *A to Z to Nairobi* is the only comprehensive guide to not only the streets in the city

but also to ministries, medical facilities, hotels, cinemas, recreational clubs and churches. Jean Hartley's *Naivasha* is a compact low-priced guide to the area.

Kathy Eldon's *Eating Out Guide to Kenya* steers the adventurous to the best food in the country, while her *Tastes of Kenya* and *Specialities of the House* provide recipes to try back home. Fatuma Shapi and Katie Halford's collection of Swahili dishes in *A Lamu Book* will give a deeper insight into that gentle cuisine.

Among Richard Leakey's books on the subject of paleontology, *Origins* and *The Making of Mankind* both give stimulating accounts on how we got where we are. How Richard Leakey got where he is, is revealed in his autobiography, *One Life*, a counter-point to his mother, Mary Leakey's autobiography, *Disclosing the Past*. Dr. Louis Leakey's own story is told in *White African*, a revealing account of the early days of Kenya.

To learn more about East Africa's recent history, Charles Miller's *Lunatic Express* is recommended, as well as his *Battle for the Bundu* which takes the reader through the First World War. Leda Farrant's *The Legendary Grogan* is an entertaining biography of one of Kenya's most illustrious white settlers, others of whom gained notoriety in the lively "Happy Valley" days of Kenya. Their antics (including the murder of a Lord) are documented in *White Mischief* by James Fox. *West With the Night*, a haunting and brilliantly written autobiography by Beryl Markham, tells of love and loss on the African plains, as does Isak Dinesen's *Out of Africa*, the basis of the film of the same name starring Meryl Streep and Robert Redford. While all these settlers were eking out a living on their farms, Jomo Kenyatta was thinking about Independence for Kenya. His *Facing Mount Kenya* is a classic which reveals the culture of the Kikuyu peoples for all to respect and understand. Jeremy Murray-Brown's biography, *Kenyatta* gives an excellent picture of the charismatic leader so inaccurately portrayed in Robert Ruark's entertaining (if distorted) books, *Something of Value* and *Uhuru*. Bringing us up to date is *The Kenyatta Succession*, Joseph Karimi and William Ochieng's description of the alleged plot to prevent Vice-President Daniel arap Moi from becoming President and how it failed.

Anyone wishing to try local contemporary novels should sample Ngugi wa Thiong'o, Kenya's best-known author who grapples with the rich-poor theme, as does David Mailu in *Down River Road*.

Andrew Fedders and Cynthia Salvadori have produced a handy series of profiles on the main tribes of Kenya under the theme, *Peoples of Kenya* and a look at the Asian community in *Through Open Doors*, while Shiva Naipul (V.S.'s brother) takes a more critical look at not only Africans but also Europeans and Asians in his fluently written *North of South* which chronicles his journey through East Africa.

Finally, just for fun, take home *Kangas, 101 Uses*, a practical and very amusing guide to the history and wearability of kangas, the most versatile piece of fabric ever invented. Written and illustrated by Jeannette Hanby and David Bygott it will keep you entertained long after memories of your Kenyan safari have faded.

THIS SPORTING LIFE

Brian Tetley

Freelance journalist and author of many
Africana books including Cradle of Mankind

Just name the sport... Kenya's probably got it. From jogging and cross-country running with the Hashhouse Harriers to scuba diving with the Sub Aqua Club in the warm waters of the Indian Ocean, Kenya offers a selection of varied pursuits unlikely to be matched by many other countries in the world. Once, someone even thought of skiing down the perilous slopes of Mount Kenya, but the logistics unfortunately excluded this sport from the list of possibilities.

Clubs, associations and informal groups, many under the aegis of the Kenya National Sports Council, keep alive and flourishing a wealth of activity ranging from the superb to the sublime—and occasionally, the ridiculous. There are more than 50 different forms of organised sport in Kenya, many of them on a competitive basis. But even the most aggressively competitive organisations will provide friendly opponents or simply the use of their facilities for those in search of more gentle recreation.

Starting with the off-beat, "loner" recreations, a few enthusiasts have set up a group of hang glider practitioners who sail forth from their favourite sites on the western edge of the Ngong Hills near Nairobi, and an escarpment on a ranch at Timau, high on the prairie shoulders of Mount Kenya. Highland thermals, sweeping in from the northern deserts below, provide a bracing wind and almost guaranteed lift-off any day of the year.

Higher up the same mountain and in streams northeast of Meru, southwest of Embu and northwest of Kiganjo, across the Laikipia Plains and on a dozen streams in the Aberdares, fly-fishermen indulge their passion for the gamest of small fish. For lesser fry (though not in size), the lure of black bass and tilapia offers a relaxing day on Naivasha's often ruffled waters while giant Nile perch provide a challenge to fishermen in Lake Victoria and Lake Turkana. The Jade Sea, though difficult and costly to reach, offers a mixture of fishing experiences including the leisure of freshwater fishing and the thrill of deepsea fishing. Tiger Fish provide fierce resistence on this exotic inland sea's turbulent waters.

Big game fishing is most easily indulged at the coast where half a dozen clubs offer all you need to enjoy the tepid Indian Ocean, teeming with everything from baracuda and sailfish to vicious sharks trolling in the dark blue waters.

Back on Mount Kenya, some of the world's most difficult ice climbs make it a shrine for serious Alpine and Himalayan climbers. All the real challenges begin well above 12,000 feet (3,694 metres) with Batian (17,058 feet/5,230 metres) and its twin peak, Nelion, the craggy spires to which all aspire. Less professional climbers can be content with conquering Point Lenana, a challenging but manageable walk with breath-taking views as the final reward.

Rock climbs are found throughout Kenya, with particularly good routes at Hell's Gate in Naivasha, in the Chyulu Hills, around Hunter's

Lodge, in the Suswa Volcano near Longonot in the Rift Valley and on Mount Elgon. Information on all types of climbing can be obtained from the Mountain Climbing Club of Kenya, based at Wilson Airport. They also have advice on another "loner" sport—parachuting—practised by a small group of enthusiasts whose brightly coloured chutes are most visible late Sunday afternoons.

Equestrian pursuits are many and varied. Kenya participates in international polo competitions, practising on their own grounds next to Jamhuri Park. Not far from the Polo Club is the beautiful tree-lined Jockey Club where alternate Sundays the "Sport of Kings" draws a large crowd who take full advantage of the betting and catering facilities at bargain prices.

Casual horse riding is possible on pony trekking safaris through the Great Rift Valley (ask any travel agent), or camelback desert safaris in the desolate north. Several stables rent horses by the hour for a hack through the forests outside of Nairobi or Mombasa.

The Aero Club of East Africa at Wilson Airport provides excellent clubhouse and swimming facilities and will gladly provide information on flying lessons and plane rentals.

Shooting is another popular pastime in Kenya, and local sportsmen compete in the Commonwealth Games, Olympics and at Bisley. Details of events, facilities and membership can be obtained through the Kenya Rifle Association near Kenyatta Hospital.

Sailing enthusiasts can choose from a variety of waters to enjoy this most graceful of sports. The quiet lagoons and creeks of Kilifi and Watamu provide a relaxing outing, while the variable waters of Lake Naivasha and Lake Victoria provide a better challenge for experienced sailers. The Nairobi Sailing Club organises jolly events at the Nairobi Dam located off the Langata Road, the first right turn after Wilson Airport.

Hot-air ballooning has had its grand moments in Kenya ever since an American film magnate arrived in 1909 complete with balloons and movie making equipment. His epic experienced a setback when the balloon with its ballast of braying donkeys broke loose from its moorings and vanished along the Rift Valley, never to be seen again.

Since then, photographer Alan Root and other intrepid souls have pursued the magnate's ambitions more successfully, and have inspired a new industry in the form of hot-air balloons from game lodges which provide an awesome early-morning view of wildlife. Book balloon safaris at Governor's Camp and Keekorok in the Maasai Mara.

Court games—badminton, squash, tennis, netball, basketball, volleyball—are played everywhere, as are rugby, cricket, hockey, swimming, snooker, darts, bridge, chess and athletics. Except for perhaps ice skating, bobsled races and cross-country skiing, Kenya can provide infinite opportunities for any sportsman.

Indeed, with so much to enjoy, the question is, how does anyone living in Kenya find the time to work?

USEFUL INFORMATION

Climate
If there is a perfect climate anywhere in the world, surely it is in Kenya, where temperatures on the coast average between 75° F and 85° (24° C to 29° C). Although it can be hot and sticky by the sea, inland the air is dry and even at midday the temperatures are quite bearable. Kenya's position on the equator means sunrise occurs daily between 6.00 and 6.30 a.m., while sunset takes place 12 hours later—just like a shade being drawn over the sky. When it's dark, the temperature drops dramatically, and visitors should pack a sweater for evenings. There are two rainy seasons—usually mid-April to the end of May, and November to mid-December. Even during the rains, the weather can be pleasant, with rain occurring early in the morning and late in the afternoon or evening.

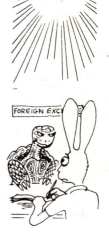

Banks
Banks can be frustrating. Service, though generally cordial, can seem highly inefficient to the visitor who must allow up to one hour to change a traveller's cheque. Banking hours are from 9.30 to 14.30 weekdays, with banks open from 9.00 to 11.00 on the first and last Saturdays of the month. There are Bureau de Change facilities in Nairobi and Mombasa which are open throughout the day. Enquire at the hotel for details.

Currency
Everyone arriving in Kenya must fill in a currency declaration form which must be turned in on departure. Each time money is changed at a bank, the transaction is recorded. Never change money on the "black market", as it is not only illegal but also highly dangerous. Check on the official exchange rate when you arrive in the country, and whenever possible change money in banks because hotels and lodges give a worse rate than banks. There are 100 cents to a shilling. Brassy yellow coins are worth five or ten cents, while fifty-cent coins, one shilling and five shillings pieces are silver. There are notes worth five, ten, twenty, fifty, Hundred, Two Hundred and Five Hundred shillings. Defacing Kenyan currency is a jailable offence so treat the money with respect! Kenya currency is "soft" and therefore not convertible abroad. Only a maximum of Hundred Shillings may be taken out of Kenya on departure.

Customs
New arrivals to Kenya may bring in personal effects, though declared gifts may be charged duty. Anyone intending to import ammunition or firearms should obtain clearance in advance. Departing visitors will have to clear customs and must not take out any illegal merchandise such as game trophies—ivory, skins, giraffe tail bracelets or bones.

Diplomatic Representation
Nearly every country has diplomatic representation in Kenya, with information on the location of embassies and consulates available in hotels or in the Kenya telephone directory. Most embassies have a 24-hour number to be called in case of emergencies.

All these new pockets...empty!

Dress

Informal is the keyword in Kenya, where style is "what feels good". Women should avoid wearing tight trousers which might offend local taste. Loose cotton trousers, skirts and shirts are ideal for shopping in Nairobi or wearing on safari, with a nice pants suit or dress perfect for evenings in the lodges. If visiting the Mount Kenya Safari Club, women should pack a dressy outfit, and men must bring a jacket and tie for the evening. Safari outfitters in Nairobi and Mombasa will provide instant new wardrobes for the chic traveller who wants to "do it right", but T-shirts and jeans are just as appropriate. Sandals are fine for travelling in a mini-bus, but sturdy footwear is essential for walking or hiking safaris. A hat is essential for everyone. The tropical sun is deceptive and burns all but the most acclimatised. Sunglasses make life much more pleasant—buy them before you come because they are expensive in Kenya.

Food and Drink

"Eat, drink and make merry" should be your motto in Kenya, a country of diverse cuisine. If you're worried, ask for a gamma globulin injection as protection against hepatitis, but most tourists will find the standards of hygiene in hotels and lodges similar to those back home. Salads are safe in the international hotels and lodges, and the water is safe from taps in Nairobi and Mombasa, though elsewhere one should ask before drinking. Most hotels and lodges provide Thermos containers of filtered water for their guests to use. Local beer, Kenya Cane and Kenya Gold liqueurs are excellent, while Papaya wine is quite acceptable and an interesting novelty for newcomers.

Health

Although no immunisations are now required to enter Kenya from Europe or the United States, it is wise to have a yellow fever vaccination, and many doctors recommend cholera and typhoid as a precaution. A hepatitis jab is advisable for adventurous eaters. Anti-malaria tablets are essential for travellers to Kenya (although malaria is not too common in Nairobi and the higher altitudes, it is advisable to be precautious). Ideally, they should be started one week before arrival in a malarial area and continued for six weeks after departure. Over-the-counter drugs can be purchased in chemist shops in the cities, and there are well-qualified doctors who can prescribe medication. Sign on with the Flying Doctors Service (Wilson Airport) which will organise emergency medical care wherever you are. The Aga Khan Hospital and Nairobi Hospital can deal with emergency cases. Remember, the sun is dangerous on the equator. Travel with the appropriate tanning or blocking lotion and creams for sunburn. A basic medicine kit should include: aspirin, Dramamine (for motion sickness), anti-diarrhoea medicine, antibiotic cream for cuts and scratches, throat lozenges, band-aids (plasters), scissors, tweezers, needle and thread, eye lotion for tired eyes and insect repellent.

Language
Although Swahili and English are the official languages of Kenya, most people speak at least one other language such as Luo, Kikuyu or Maasai. Learning a few words of Swahili will win an instant smile and take you out of the ordinary tourist category.

hello	*jambo*
how are you?	*habari?*
fine	*nzuri*
thank you	*asante*
very much	*sana*
please	*tafadhali*
goodbye	*kwaheri*

Manners
Kenyans are friendly people. You're always safe with the greeting "jambo" and the instant response of "mzuri" (fine), even if you're not. Everyone shakes hands at every opportunity, so cultivate the habit. Ask before photographing anyone and never photograph Maasai or Samburu people without obtaining permission (usually given if you pay a fee in advance). Kenyans are proud of their country, so don't offend them by insensitive critical remarks.

Security
Act in Nairobi as you would in New York, London or Paris. Watch your handbag or wallet carefully and conceal valuable jewellery, gold chains or expensive watches beneath your clothes while walking on the streets. Place valuables in the hotel safe and carry only what you don't mind losing. Don't change money illegally—it's asking for trouble, and do be very careful on lonely beaches.

Shopping
For detailed information read the chapter on what to buy. Shop hours are generally from 8.30 to 12.30 and from 14.00 to 17.30 **Mondays to Fridays**, and 8.30 to 12.30 on Saturdays, although shops for tourists may stay open through the lunch hour and later in the evening. Even when the sign says "fixed price" it's worth a friendly attempt at bargaining, and in markets and kiosks, bargaining is *de rigeur*. Imported items are expensive in Kenya; they are subject to high duties and sales tax—so save those purchases for your return. Take advantage of good local buys such as hand-crafted items and printed material which are bargains.

Sport
For a detailed survey read the chapter entitled "This Sporting Life" by Brian Tetley. Take advantage of good golf courses while in Kenya, as well as inexpensive horse-riding, camel-safaris and mountain climbing. Visitors to the coast should sample the delights of skin-diving, deepsea fishing, water-skiing, sailing, surfing, goggling or scuba diving. All the

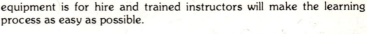

equipment is for hire and trained instructors will make the learning process as easy as possible.

Telephones, Post and Telegraph
Except during the rains, the telephone system is fairly reliable in Kenya. International calls can be direct-dialled or operator-assisted by dialling 0196. Beware of making trunk calls in hotels, where a hefty charge is often added to the bill. Dialling from a pay phone isn't as confusing as it appears—simply place the coin in the hole provided and dial. The coin will drop automatically when the phone is answered. When addressing a letter within Kenya, note that there are no street addresses, only box numbers. Stamps, air letters and telegraph facilities are available in post offices. External telex facilities are also available in the major cities.

Tipping
A service charge is included in the bill in hotels and lodges, but tipping is expected on bar service—usually 10% of the bill is sufficient. Tip waiters between 5% and 10% at restaurants where a service is not included on the bill. Drivers of Safari vehicles should be tipped approximately Kshs. 50 per passenger per day. Hotel/airport porters expect about Kshs. 5 per suitcase.

Visas
A valid visa is necessary for visitors from non-Commonwealth countries. Regulations should be checked before travelling to Kenya, as requirements vary according to country. Visitors with proper documentation holding onward or return tickets may obtain "Visitors Passes", normally valid for three months, on arrival at any Kenya port of entry. Upon departure by air from Kenya, travellers pay an airport tax (currently $20 or the equivalent in another hard currency). Travellers also pay a service charge of Kshs. 50 on all domestic flights.

SAFARI ESSENTIALS

Although you can buy just about anything in Nairobi, it's generally cheaper and easier to bring what you need from home. The exception to this rule is safari gear; bush clothes, hats and safari boots are good buys in Kenya. Unless you are visiting the Mount Kenya Safari Club, which requires a jacket and tie, men don't need a suit on safari. Clothing should be loose-fitting and very comfortable, cool for day-time wear, while evenings require a sweater or wrap of some kind. Don't bring too much on safari, it will only get in the way.

Checklist
2 kangas or kikoys
2 pairs shorts
2 pairs slacks or jeans
2-3 tee shirts or short-sleeved shirts
1 long-sleeved shirt
bush jacket or sweater
swim wear
night wear, including a bathrobe for lodges
1 pair strong walking shoes or tennis shoes
5-6 pairs socks
underwear
deep-brimmed hat
sunblock, tanning lotion, sunburn cream
basic first aid kit (see section on Health for detailed list)
basic cosmetics, shampoo and shaving supplies
battery-operated shaver
extra batteries
flashlight
100-watt push in light bulb (handy if the lodge lightbulbs are low wattage)
plug adaptors for hair drier, shaver, curlers, etc.
a few snack foods: don't go overboard as there is always too much food on safari
2 bottles soda water or mineral water for emergencies
needle and thread, soap, safety pins, small plastic bags, clothesline
cameras, extra lenses, too much film, extra batteries for flash
binoculars
fold-away carry all
sun-glasses

SAY IT IN SWAHILI

Getting Acquainted

Hello	*Jambo*
How are you?	*Habari?*
Good, very well	*Mzuri*
Bad	*Mbaya*
Thank you	*Asante*
Very much	*Sana*
Please	*Tafadhali*
What is your name?	*Jina lako nani?*
Goodbye	*Kwaheri*
Welcome	*Karibu*
Danger	*Hatari*
Friend	*Rafiki*
Shop	*Duka*
How much?	*Bei gani*
Money	*Pesa*
Expensive	*Ghali*
Bring	*lete*
A lot, many	*Nyingi*
Another	*Ngine*
Enough	*Intosha*
Now	*Sasa*

Numbers

One	*Moja*
Two	*Mbili*
Three	*Tatu*
Four	*Nne*
Five	*Tano*
Six	*Sita*
Seven	*Saba*
Eight	*Nane*
Nine	*Tisa*
Ten	*Kumi*

Getting Around

I'm lost	*Nimepotea*
Where	*Wapi?*
Why	*Kwa nini?*
When	*Lini?*
How	*Vipi?*
Let's go	*Twende*
Wait here	*Ngoja hapa*

Eating Out

Drinks	
Beer	*Pombe*
Coffee	*Kahawa*
Tea	*Chai*
Milk	*Maziwa*
Water	*Maji*
Cold	*Baridi*
Hot	*Moto*
Ice	*Barafu*
Food	*Chakula*
Eggs	*Mayai*
Meat	*Nyama*
Fish	*Samaki*
Chicken	*Kuku*
Fruit	*Matunda*
Vegetables	*Mboga*
Potatoes	*Viazi*
Rice	*Wali*
Salt	*Chumvi*
Sugar	*Sukari*

On Safari

Baboon, monkey	*Nyani*
Buffalo	*Nyati*
Cheetah	*Duma*
Elephant	*Tembo*
Giraffe	*Twiga*
Hippo	*Kiboko*
Hyena	*Fisi*
Impala	*Swara*
Leopard	*Chui*
Lion	*Simba*
Monkey	*Nyani*
Rhino	*Kifaru*
Zebra	*Punda milia*

Emergency

Help	*Saidia*
Fire	*Moto*
Thief	*Mwizi*

BIRD AND ANIMAL SPOTTER

Species	Location	Species	Location
Aardvark		Giraffe (Reticulated)	
Aaardwolf		Goliath Heron	
Baboon		Grant's Gazelle	
Bat-eared Fox		Hare	
Bongo		Hartebeest	
Buffalo		Hippopotamus	
Bush Baby		Honey Badger	
Bush Pig		Hunting Dog	
Caracal		Hyena (Spotted)	
Cheetah		Hyena (Striped)	
Civet Cat		Hyrax	
Cormorant		Impala	
Crocodile		Jackal	
Crowned-crested Crane		Klipspringer	
Dik dik		Kudu (Greater)	
Duiker		Kudu (Lesser)	
Egret		Leopard	
Egyptian Goose		Lion	
Eland		Marabou Stork	
Elephant		Mongoose	
Fish Eagle		Monitor Lizard	
Flamingo		Monkey (Colobus)	
Genet Cat		Monkey (Patas)	
Gerenuk		Monkey (Syke's)	
Giant Forest Hog		Monkey (Vervet)	
Giraffe (Maasai)		Oribi	

BIRD AND ANIMAL SPOTTER

Species	Location	Species	Location
Oryx		Spring Hare	
Ostrich		Squirrel	
Otter		Steinbok	
Pangolin		Superb Starling	
Porcupine		Suni	
Reedbuck		Thomson's Gazelle	
Rhinocerous (White)		Topi	
Rhinocerous (Black)		Vulture	
Roan Antelope		Warthog	
Sable Antelope		Waterbuck	
Sacred Ibis		Wildcat	
Secretary Bird		Wildebeest	
Serval Cat		Yellow-billed stock	
Sitatunga			

RECORD OF CURRENCY TRANSACTIONS

Date	Amount	Where Exchanged	Cheque Number	Rate	Amount Received

SHOPPING

Item	Where bought	Price

DAILY RECORD

Day 1   **Date**

Day 2   **Date**

DAILY RECORD

Day 3   Date

Day 4   Date

DAILY RECORD

Day 5   **Date**

Day 6   **Date**

DAILY RECORD

Day 7   **Date**

Day 8   **Date**

DAILY RECORD

Day 9   **Date**

Day 10   **Date**

DAILY RECORD

Day 11   **Date**

Day 12   **Date**

DAILY RECORD

Day 13   **Date**

Day 14   **Date**

DAILY RECORD

Day 15   **Date**

Day 16   **Date**

DAILY RECORD

Day 17   **Date**

Day 18   **Date**

DAILY RECORD

Day 19   **Date**

Day 20   **Date**

70

ADDRESSES

Who	Where met	Address

NOTES

NOTES

NOTES